A Voice
at the Borders of Silence

A Voice
at the Borders of Silence

*An Intimate View of
the Gurdjieff Work, Zen Buddhism, and Art*

William Segal
with
Marielle Bancou-Segal

EDITED BY MARK MAGILL

THE OVERLOOK PRESS
Woodstock & New York

First published in the United States in 2003 by
The Overlook Press, Peter Mayer Publishers, Inc.
Woodstock & New York

WOODSTOCK:
One Overlook Drive
Woodstock, NY 12498
www.overlookpress.com
[for individual orders, bulk and special sales, contact our Woodstock office]

NEW YORK:
141 Wooster Street
New York, NY 10012

PHOTO CREDITS:
David Heald: pages iv, 160, 163, 167-172, 178, 182, 186; Lee Ewing: pages iv,
68, 274, 280; Roger Sherman: pages i, v, 155, 183, 187, 229, 245, 247, 253;
Maya Deren: pages 45-46; Charles Van Maaren: page 209

PERMISSIONS
"Masters: Interview with Marvin Barrett" is reprinted by permission from
Parabola, Vol. 25, No. 3 (Fall, 2000). "Sleep: Interview with Dr. Yeshi Dhonden"
is reprinted by permission from *Parabola*, Vol. 7, No. 1 (Spring, 1982)

∞ The paper used in this book meets the requirements for paper
permanence as described in the ANSI Z39.48-1992 standard.

Library of Congress Cataloging-in-Publication Data

Segal William.
A voice at the borders of silence: an intimate view of the
Gurdjieff work, Zen Buddhism, and art / William Segal.
p. cm.
1. Segal, William. 2. Spiritual biography—United States. I. Title.
BL73.S48 A3 2003   291.4'092—b21   2003054853

Printed in the United States of America
ISBN 1-58567-442-7
FIRST EDITION
1 3 5 7 9 8 6 4 2

v

vi

Contents

Vezelay is here.

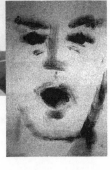

"parceque c'etait lui"

the master might be
behind the counter

painting is the devil

the old man doing nothing

The Last Word

"They are all angels," said Bill.

He was contemplating the dense crowd of depressed, distracted bodies crammed together in the Paris Metro. "They are all angels," he repeated. "But they don't know it!" This was a joke, yet in Bill's own way, it was no joke. Bill lived with and constantly perceived the reality of two worlds, two levels of existence, apparently separate one from another, to be tasted by most of us in different ways on different days. For Bill, all experience was one: sound meant silence, movement was part of stillness. There were no divisions: dividing was just a way of thinking and the emptiness where impressions arise was so close to him that he would say, touching the point of jaw where cheek meets bone "I feel it here."

So there were no contradictions among his many lives, a man of the city who was a man of nature, a shrewd and humorous businessman, the speediest American foot-baller of his decade who became an artist, a connoisseur, a poet, a painter and who remained an exquisite, immac-ulately elegant Japanese monk. His many personalities, warm, diplomatic, observant, outgoing were not mere facets. They were the fluent adjustments of the hidden man to the everyday world. How often, year after year, I would say "farewell" to Bill, as though for the last time. He would insist on coming to the elevator, holding his radiantly loving wife Marielle by the arm. As the doors slid together and I caught a final glimpse of him, I could never believe that so fragile a frame could be so tough and firm. Yet even in his final moments, the voice on the phone had the same strong and cheerful presence. When we were together for the very last time, his voice reduced to a murmur, his head deep in the pillows, he whispered with the ghost of a smile:

"A vibration somewhere . . . becomes an atom . . . a nerve . . . a piece of skin . . . and a cheek." He touches mine, and then with a tiny waving of a finger, "all this follows . . ."

For his sense of wonder was inseparable from his humor. Only when he painted did he vanish, to become just a hand, a brush, that served a seeing far beyond the normal eye. Bill was a man of many layers and if the outer layer was the man of today, the innermost core was an opening to eternity. For this, he was gifted, and yet no gift is truly given. It has to be paid for. For nearly a century Bill worked, worked on himself and selflessly worked for others, through a devotion to a rare quality of existence that he perceived and needed to share. In this way, the searcher, the artist, the pupil and the teacher became one, humbly, with simplicity.

Of all the many images of Bill that I cherish, from my secret collection of photographs whether on paper or in the mind, one always comes to the fore. It is Bill peering at me quizzically saying: "What's it all about? . . . What do you think? . . . What's it all about? . . ." I could feel that he meant this as the deepest of human questions. The life of the spirit might hang on the answer, yet over-seriousness would kill it dead. Life is to be lived, with laughter and astonishment.

"What were his last words?" people ask. Of course. We want to know. But the answer is not to be found in a single unforgettable phrase. The memory of Bill as he was at any moment in life was and remains his first and last word, a word that is uniquely his own.

—Peter Brook

Foreword

by Robert Thurman

Bill Segal was constantly amazed by the universe, wonder was his middle name. At the same time his presence was humble and unassuming. His favorite approach to conversation was to ask a question. Often when I would visit him in later days, after hospitable greetings and hugs and sittings down he would look at me with an open smile and ask the cosmic question, "What's it all about Bob?" Most lately he would often ask, "Do you really think there is some sort of further life? What do you think it really means to say that?"

He would always entertain whatever I would say with great seriousness, as if the traditional ideas or my renderings of them at that moment were entirely new to him. He would then reflect his exquisite integration of insightful uncertainty and eager open-mindedness and we would come to a restful silence, until the sweep of a more general conversation with others would pick us up. Though what our Zen friends would call "the stink of enlightenment" sometimes seemed to swirl around him, his own discipline of concentrating on a dominant inner silence, a space of abstention from rigid self notions, seemed to make him immune to any taint of claiming such a position.

As amazed as he always was about life, I often found him rewardingly surprising. I guess he surprised me most strongly three times. The first time was early on in my rediscovery of Bill, when he and Marielle and a young photographer friend visited my place in the country to interview his Holiness, the Dalai Lama's personal physician, Dr. Yeshi Dhonden. I was the doctor's interpreter for the conversation. Everyone sat down comfortably. The tape was put on and Bill began. I expected some sort of cosmic question, a probing of the great diagnostician, the learned healer.

Bill asked, "What is the meaning of sleep?"

As interpreter I could not interfere. But I was startled and thought it a waste, to focus on such a commonplace item. But Dr.Dhoden didn't miss a beat, and launched into a discussion of the homology between sleep, death, clear light, ultimate reality, and the Truth Body of all Buddhas! I was surprised and humbled. Sleep was indeed profound in meaning. I had previously learned most of what the doctor was saying, so I easily translated it. But I had left it in the topic learned, and somehow had not connected it in the everyday continuum with the mundane activity of sleeping.

The second big surprise Bill handed me was from his charcoal drawings, which aptly got called "Transparencies." Simple black and white, still lives of table objects, especially glasses, emerged in the luminosity of enlightened perception. Ultimate experience of this is called "clear light," which is often misunderstood to refer to a bright white light. But the white light is a more superficial level of reality, the moonlit level called "luminance." The clear light is just transparency, compared to the gray dawn twilight when you can see your hand but not the lines in it. It is a light that does not fall on objects, but comes from within them, casting no shadows. It is a self-luminous, non-dual awareness and presence. And Bill, untroubled by the sophisticated Tibetan phenomenology of such states, was bringing it into our dualistic awareness by scratching on paper with bits of charcoal. I was awestruck.

The third surprise came after Bill died. At the funeral, which occurred in the same funeral parlor on 81st Street where my father's funeral took place, I learned that Bill had admired very much the lines of the Japanese Heian Buddhist poet, Saigyo.

> My prayer is to die underneath the
> Blossoming cherry,
> In that spring month of flowers,
> When the moon is full.

For Saigyo it was a great honor to die on the very day the

Japanese celebrate as the Parinirvana or blissful death day of Shakyamuni Buddha. They associated it with Mt. Yoshino, where profuse cherry blossoms fall unusually on that full moon day in May. It is even said that Saigyo lived up to his poem, and did pass away that very day in a later year, without any artificial assistance. How exquisite and how instructive for us, that such a great adept could attune his life rhythms, so that he could use his own death moment to participate in the supreme bliss of final release of the most evolved of all beings.

Bill had never mentioned his love for this poem in particular. He certainly was tired of his body long before he died, and might have passed over on many occasions during the long winter before, for all of Marielle's loving ministrations. A funny feeling gripped me. Sitting there at Frank Campbell's on 81st Street and Madison, I counted back the days to Bill's death. It was the month of May. He had died on the full moon day, when the cherry blossoms on Mt. Yoshino must have been falling in all their delicate glory, and hundreds of millions of Buddhists the world over open their minds joyfully to the enlightenment and final release of the great Lord of Bliss!

Quiet harbinger of enlightenment in the West! True man of no rank! Roaming the market place with open hands! Hail to Bill!

Introduction
"Presence de Bill"

As a witness to this life of vivid colors, a variety of occupations and meetings with notable friends, I often pushed my husband, William Segal, to write his autobiography. He was not completely against it. We had even given a name to it: Nine Decades.

Although he insisted on the vanity—indeed the total uselessness—of the kind of exercise an autobiography represents, when we had the time and the calm, often at Chester, our country house, Bill never refused to tell me about the various periods of his life. I would ask short questions. He would reply at length and with pleasure, smiling at his past. So we taped our sessions in no special order other than vaguely chronological. They were mainly about the beginnings of his life, the times I did not know. After the notes were transcribed, Bill would edit them, a work that was fascinating to watch. With the total attention he so often recommended and brought to whatever he undertook, he would eliminate two-thirds of the spoken narrative. This is why some chapters are short; some may look incomplete. They are the result of meandrous conversations at Chester, during snowy nights.

He was the new man, "avant-garde" American of the twentieth century, a curious and open spirit involved in business and art, philosophy and physics, religion and money.

He was avant-garde in his most original publishing enterprises; he sent his daughters to avant-garde schools; he had his offices and apartments decorated by Alvin Lustig, the most modern designer of the '50s. Avant-garde in his taste for cars: he often spoke of his Chrysler 300 as of a favorite art object. Above all, he was avant-garde in his spiritual life, first following P.D. Ouspensky, who introduced him to the world of Gurdjieff and the leading edge of the New Age of that time. Bill came to know D.T. Suzuki, who was lecturing at Columbia University and was one of the Zen pioneers of America. He also visited H.H. the Dalaï Lama in his early days in Dharamsala.

In some traditions, biography is a high form of literature. It is used to tell the story of a life that offers a perfect model to the reader. The expression "perfect model" would have sounded totally false to this man of deep humility, who found simply natural whatever he was undertaking. But he might have accepted the idea of being avant-garde.

In this exceptionally gifted human being—active, engaged and engaging—two features stand out: the constant ascending movement of transformation, and the presence, always. It is difficult to believe in "horizontal" progress, as a line of historical time, when one has witnessed the carnage of the twentieth century. Nevertheless, individual vertical progress seems to take place when one looks at Bill's evolution in twentieth century America, when it was possible to break through to new levels very quickly. One could climb the economic, social and spiritual ladder in a single generation.

But to go further and faster, a shock was needed. It was sent to Bill in the form of the horrendous car accident that, in 1971, put him within a hairsbreadth of losing his life and brought him face to face with death. While he was recovering, his friend Soen Nakagawa, abbot of Ryutaku-ji, visited him. "Lucky man," said the roshi, "One accident like yours is worth 10,000 sittings in a monastery."

The acceleration of the transformation was spectacular. "I have a different face," said Bill. The new person was different from the one who had avidly taken everything on board, doing ceaselessly, always moving ahead.

Another part of the book consists of serious conversations with friends, and it is still Bill's voice one hears. Most of the talks took place in the last 15 years of his life. The various subjects treated were always linked to his inward search. We did not place them chronologically, but in chapters where their themes correspond. For instance, the exchanges with painters on art are part of a long chapter, "The Painter." Bill often repeated "I painted all my life," and said to a friend, "Painting is the devil." He was always carrying a sketch book, drawing an object, the face of a friend, a landscape. But the core of his spiritual search was strongly linked to his self-portraits. In

1999, Bill's last exhibition in New York, at Tibet House, had for its title: "60 Years of Self-portraits as Self-search." And he kept on his desk a letter from his friend Peyton Houston, commenting on this self-portraiture (Peyton was a poet and a president of large corporations):

"I have been thinking about your question on self-portraiture. Isn't it perhaps because the 'self' is the most mysterious thing in the universe and most crucial to get at the riddle of the simple is, so that we must challenge and investigate to take off the hidings and wrappings and penetrate (perhaps) to the resident angel there? What am I? Who am I? are essential parts to what I call the ontological predicament of 1st) being, and 2nd) of being human. I am sure Rembrandt had this in all those searching studies. What clearer road is there to the spiritual challenge? And, further, and as with all important things in the arts, it is to deal with the directions given by the deep instinct."

"The neglected stranger" was the name Bill gave to this hidden self. He wrote: "The discovery of the neglected stranger is really the aim of our existence. We are in a position where we cannot entirely approach the entity intellectually or philosophically. The mysterious entity, this stranger, has to be grasped by experience."

Ken Burns, modern historian of America, created a trilogy of films on three aspects of Bill's life. The first, "William Segal," is on the painter. The second, "Vezelay," shows the searcher meditating in the crypt of the basilique. The old man "In the Market Place," the third film, was inspired by the presence of Bill, so intense in his last years. This film is presented through the Chinese symbol of the 10 oxherdings story: In the 10th and final picture, the old man, by his presence alone, enlightens those he meets. Before each film, Ken did long interviews with Bill and those three conversations are included in this book.

It is difficult to be both involved and objective, which is the situation in which a wife finds herself as she shapes her husband's autobiography. However, throughout the chapters of this book, made up of various documents, it is always the autobiographical voice which is heard, in the interviews, conversations and letters. But sometimes a second voice, that of the wife, is added in parallel.

The years we were together were spent in a new atmosphere, the presence of the couple. We came to know each other when Bill was sixty-five; I was fifty. My son Pascal was pursuing a work-study program between semesters, as required by his college. He had been directed to American Fabrics, the famous textile magazine. The editors, Mr. and Mrs. Segal, had been very open and helpful, and Pascal asked me to invite them to dine. I did so, but it was not a great feast of mutual sympathy.

A little later, Cora Segal died. The year before, I had lost the father of my son, my companion of more than twenty years. Bill said that my letter of condolence really touched him, among the many he received. He invited me to lunch. He had found me some work in Japan and thought we should discuss it. Then he left for extensive travels in India. We kept in touch by mail.

Some months later, I saw him at the Good Samaritan Hospital after his car wreck. The accident had rendered him so unrecognizable that one of his friends fainted on seeing his enormously swollen, inhuman-looking face. The calm sureness of his will was admirable. A tracheotomy prevented him from speaking. So he wrote what he wanted to say on a pad of yellow paper. I remember one sentence: "God is a terrible being."

Bill remained in the hospital for several months, enduring fourteen operations. One evening, when I was beside him, he finally exploded, "Take me out of here, now!"

I accompanied him home in the ambulance to Sixty-ninth Street. He was silent and very present. I had more or less taken charge of organizing life in his apartment: hospital bed, nurse, cook. Each time I came back from my work in Tokyo or Paris I kept him company. For hours and hours he would practice the exercises he had been advised to do.

We were married in 1972, without a ceremony, without a synagogue for Bill, without a Rumanian Orthodox church for me. City Hall, then a glass of champagne with dear friends.

We lived together for almost for almost thirty years. And

when I say "together," I mean you could count on your fingers the few weeks that were lived separately. In those thirty years, we felt no need to celebrate one day more than another. We liked what Heraclitus said, "One day is like all the rest." Every day together was a feast day.

—Marielle Bancou-Segal

I the question of search

Vezelay at the top of the hill

Vezelay Is Here

A Conversation with Ken Burns

KB: Mr. Segal, we've engaged a question of search. Why do we search?

WCS: There is the strange fact that we've been drawn here to this meeting, and we can't say why we search except that there seems to be an innate need, or an innate call in each human being, more or less strong, stronger in one than in another. But this need, this call to search, is to know who one is, what we're here for, what our destiny is, how to live more poetically.

KB: There's something unsatisfying about our daily lives. Do we begin to realize that our daily lives don't provide something that we need?

WCS: It isn't that our daily lives are not satisfactory. It is that the fact that we don't have, we don't include in our daily lives, that element of the light, of God, if you wish, or a higher note, a higher energy, which should accompany our daily lives. It's we who corrupt, spoil, change them, live in them in an unbecoming way. This is the way I see it.

KB: So I am not me.

WCS: Believe me, none of us know who we are, and this search to know who we are seems to be, as I've said before, innate in each human being. At the same time, no matter what level or what stage we're at, we have the feeling that we're part of a great scheme, a great drama, where each one contributes and is part of the drama.

KB: How does one search?

WCS: Right now the search begins when one is present to something. It sounds very vague, something in one's self that's relatively changeless, that's always here. We know that our minds change at each moment, our bodies are always changing, our desires, our wishes, our prejudices. But underneath there is the feeling

of "I," a reality which is not subject to the change which ordinarily characterizes our lives. One must think from one's own experience and find that relationship with one's self that gives a kind of a new joyousness, a new freedom, a new way of living as part of a great universe.

KB: What in our ordinary lives brings us to this search?

WCS: If we are able to satisfy our so-called desires, if fate or circumstance grants our wishes and if we have been endowed with superb health, beauty, money, possessions, relationships, love, at least for some people it seems that there's a call for something else. From a sensual point of view, people who pander to their bodies, their appetites, no matter how much they eat, how they choose their food, it's not enough. Sensual pleasures pall after a while. Everything comes to its opposite. We find that love doesn't last. The divorce rate of our modern society is horrendous. Nothing is forever. There is, I think, a natural call, "Well, what is there, that would truly meet my heart's desire, truly make me freer, happier, more in tune with what life seems to be all about?" Eventually the search begins with the realization that I don't know myself. "Who am I?" becomes a burning question. I know I am going to die and at the same time I have a feeling that I am here for something. The search begins at this point, I believe, with the quest to know who we are, what we are here for, where we're going, what our possibilities are. And inevitably, when the question arises, the answers gradually begin to come, and the obstacles come too. I find that I can't concentrate on

this question, I'm like a reed in the wind, shifted. First this attracts me, then something else attracts me. So, I may meet somebody, or I may read a book, or go to my church or temple, or I'm touched by something in nature, in a child, in a face, in a relationship, and I begin to have an inkling of a presence in me of some element that can change the equation of having and not having. Saying yes and then no, being torn between desires. I feel that we are all here for something, that we are part of a conscious upward movement, spiral movement, conscious transformation. And so my search begins to take more concrete form.

KB: As it takes more concrete form, what are the steps . . .

WCS: In a practical sense, I would say, it's a question of openness, being sensitive to what is in one and what is around one. We live rather indrawn lives, selfishly, inward, directed only on me, mine. Then I begin to see that there is something else in the equation of life and that something else touches sensitive parts of myself and beckons me to a still further search, to know still more. I find that my capacity to be open is rather limited. I find that I don't have the mental equipment, the knowledge that is needed to deepen and make the search truly effective.

KB: I've been thinking about Vezelay. Can a place, like a great cathedral, aid in our search, help our search?

WCS: It's better to be at Vezelay than to be at a discotheque if one is serious about oneself. At the same

time, it is not the place, it's the places in the interior of oneself. There are forces around a place like Vezelay which remind one. There is a stillness here, the silence, the call of the sound of the bells. People are at their best here. They are not as preoccupied and not as combative, not the way they are in ordinary life. We do change with the place. But truly the idea of search is connected very often with shock, with sorrow, with the arousing of something in one's conscience, with tragedy. Or it could be an illumination, through seeing something in nature. To go back to Vezelay, I think it's good to place oneself in what might be called advantageous circumstances, but eventually it doesn't make any difference. I always like the idea of the man in the marketplace, just an ordinary

man walking around, and he's searching in the middle of the clamor of the people speaking, shouting. That's interesting to me. Because for me at least, the search continues wherever one is.

KB: What draws us to Vezelay?

WCS: Some people feel a true need to be in touch with what's not their ordinary existence. Other people come for sightseeing. I can't say. What brought you here, what brought me here? I recall years ago, someone said that Vezelay was a holy place. Well, I go to any holy place if I am able to. We like to see order, places where there is physical order, there's evidence of symmetry, there's evidence of beauty, there's evidence of a harmonious reflection of man's capacities. Vezelay, with its, beauty is one of those places.

KB: Is there something already here on this mountain, or is this thing that we feel at Vezelay something that man has added over the years?

WCS: Over the hundreds of years people have come here with their best intentions, with what we might call "good vibrations." These deposits are felt, just as one feels the atmosphere of a prison or of a place where crimes have been committed. We feel the beneficent atmosphere and perhaps the location, on top of a mountain.

KB: But in the end it's really not about Vezelay, is it?

WCS: Vezelay is here, inside of one. You create Vezelay in this moment. If one remembers, "Be still, and know that I am," Vezelay is here. As soon as I become angry, violent, filled with egoism, Vezelay moves away.

KB: As we observe the simple Roman Catholic rituals at Vezelay, the question is, how does daily ritual help us in our search?

WCS: When one is here, at this Catholic holy place, one is aware that one is. After all, people have dedicated themselves to living more becomingly, to be mindful,

and so we can't help but be affected by this particular place, this atmosphere, built over centuries.

KB: And their daily rituals, are they reminders?

WCS: You've used the right word. Some people disdain ritual, but to some people, every moment is a ritual. Every gesture can be a ritual. I have my morning coffee, it could be a ritual. Greeting, seeing you is a ritual. Walking, turning, breathing is a ritual. It's a giving and receiving. But the ritual as delineated by a church is a very concrete reminder, it brings you back. Every ritual is a reminder. At the same time one has to be aware of the danger of the ritual becoming mechanical. One goes through motions with very little content, and I'm afraid that does happen in many places. But it is up to each one of us to make the ritual meaningful.

KB: What about music? Can music aid in this search, and how do I take in music that might awaken something?

WCS: Music might be considered a kind of a shock which opens. One can be more receptive. Music is a gift from heaven which comes and helps to open up the human being to what he is not, as well as to what he is.

KB: How do we listen to music, how could we listen to music, not just with our ears?

WCS: Music may be a step, a milestone on the way to be able to listen to a universal sound. This universal sound in oneself, this listening, is an integral part of the search. When I listen to good music, I'm listening with all parts of myself. I may be taking the first steps towards listening to a voice coming from a higher place. And it connects, perhaps, with this idea of "be still and know that I am." I have to be able to listen with great attention, and this level of listening calls for an ability to maintain a relationship with the silence. This necessity in turn indicates that we're in mechanical movement, never allowing for the supreme relation. And listening to music may be the first step towards listening to another level of life.

KB: Is quiet and meditation a prerequisite for our search?

WCS: Eventually one has to come to appreciate and to give more time to being quiet and to meditation. On the other hand, one has to acknowledge that the whole idea of search entails a process. When one speaks of meditation, one has to take into the account the preparation to be able to meditate. Most people's minds and feelings run away with them. We associate rather than think. We react rather than feel in a true way. And to be able to meditate means to be able to withdraw part of this associative thinking. This requires a concentration and an ability to be here in this moment of now, listening, letting something enter which we ordinarily block away from ourselves.

KB: There is a good deal of religious symbolism, specific in this case to the Roman Catholic Church, at Vezelay. And we seem to be inspired, indeed shocked, in moments, at details, as we look around here. That returns us to the idea of luminosity.

WCS: Even the humblest church or temple has something holy about it. They provide the shock which brings one to a stop and makes possible the opening to something quite different from the ordinary. On the other hand, the work of the artist, the human face, the humblest flower arrangement or vegetable arrangement, or even an ash heap, seen with a certain vision, can also provide this shock. It always comes back to you, to me, to the human being. One has to be able to give oneself an inner stop. When one stops, it's a shock, and it is as if something opens up. The process of evolutionary transformation can then take place.

KB: When you speak about quiet, about what one brings, you are talking about living a principled life. Vezelay reminds us that we have that possibility.

WCS: We need Vezelay, we need the churches, the temples, the mountains. We need nature, we need the children's faces, we need relationships with each other. But, finally, God is everywhere. Especially when one stops for a moment and listens, something appears which illuminates and vivifies, changes and transforms. It always comes back to oneself.

KB: What is the role of resistance? What is the attitude that one needs to have in relationship to the friction that inevitably arises?

WCS: When I see conflicting desires in myself, when I see the resistance, when I see the movement in an unbecoming direction, it makes me turn. There is a law of gravity, of a downward pull. A constant watchfulness is required because the forces that put one to sleep are here. I mean the gender of the body, the senses, all have their agenda which calls for them to be, to eat and to take care of themselves. Each part of our body wants something from nature because this is part of a universal scheme which we don't really understand. In this scheme of the universe, the human being has his unique role of transforming the elements of nature in the direction of more and more consciousness. Human beings do not always realize this role, but they are bound to fulfill it anyway.

KB: The usefulness of such sacred places as Vezelay is in the shock of reminding us.

WCS: Yes, they're reminders. If we didn't have a Vezelay, we would have created Vezelay because something in the human being knows there's a necessity to have a reminder. We come to the realization that we need to be helped. The Vezelays of the world help us.

KB: As a painter, as you move around Vezelay, what is it that you look at, what do you drink in here?

WCS: Vezelay is different from most places because it has the virtue of being isolated, closer to nature, closer to the sky, to the open heavens. Everything here is created with a certain reverence, with attention, love and respect, whereas things that we ordinarily see in the cities are rather commercialized.

KB: I'm thinking about luminosity and Vezelay and this idea of shock, a place like this could wake us up.

WCS: We come back to the question of search. Search is both solitary and shared, and when one comes to Vezelay, one feels the beginnings of an impulse towards sharing with others. But it's so difficult. I notice on the faces of the visitors, the attitudes, the movements of the visitors, including ourselves, we cannot seem to shake the old habits of a me, mine, selfishness. We're not so egocentric as we are in our ordinary environment. The building itself, the mass, the way the people are, the stones of this place, speak of a sharing. This, in a way, is very alien to our modern life.

KB: With this question of search foremost in our minds, can we do it alone?

WCS: Yes. Each individual is different. Every one of us will and does take a different path. But relationships with each other are very important because we are all part of the ultimate and the profound vibration. So we can never dispense with relationship and retreat into our own little ivory tower.

KB:: What feeds search?

WCS: More search. The more one searches, the more one discovers. It's like love. Love, my wife says, multiplies. The experience itself cannot be discounted. All of these feelings of being, of shaking off the bondage of my ordinary small self, make me hungry for a little more. I have to see that I'm being pulled this way and that way, and to feed that little flame which is eventually growing into the important element.

KB: You speak of the higher a lot. What is it in us that relates to the higher?

WCS: The higher itself. In each one of us there is the highest. Man has rightfully been said to contain all the elements of the universe. And he contains the subtlest, finest, swiftest vibration that can be sensitive to the beauties around us, to the potentialities for more vivid living, for more openness. Light is better than darkness, isn't it? Beauty is better than selfish ugliness.

KB: Does the search ever end?

WCS: There's no ending that a human being could visualize, or can comprehend. I could contemplate a state of being where I am in continual ecstasy, but why would I want to be in continual ecstasy? At the same time, I think it is the destiny of human beings to be free, open, generous, poetical, giving, loving, hospitable, serene, intelligent, instead of being pulled down by forces which make them dull and selfish. But I'm not a philosopher.

KB: I think you answered the next question I was going to ask you. What do we find when we search?

WCS: Again, it may sound presumptuous, but being an old man I can say that one finds a network of unity, of oneness. I am not separated from you, or from the animals, from the insects, or even from the stone, from nature. One finds truly a oneness with all things. But I don't know whether these are just words, "I am," this wonderful phrase, "I am." Just this is-ness is wonderful. I don't have to say I am something—I am. That's enough. One finds this "I am-ness" through the silence. The silence is, the nothingness is filled with everything. I can't answer some questions. Words are not very adequate to express what one might find. One finds this moment. One finds your smile.

KB: I'd like to come back to the beginning. The first question, what is search?

WCS: Search really begins with seeing the obstructions, the obstacles, the barriers in the way of enabling us to be what we essentially are. And what is not realized sufficiently is that search is no different than a becoming, as one becomes a lawyer, a doctor, a musician, a painter, a financier, an economist, a truck driver, a cook. One has to know how to search. Here we come to the necessity of being able to concentrate in the same way that if I wish to be a good baker I have to concentrate on baking. In search, one is faced with the necessity of concentrating one's entire attention on this small, weak-voiced element in oneself that's crying to be heard. Crying in the wilderness. Search entails recognition of the distractions in the way of looking, of seeing. So perhaps one could come to a definition of search in the sense that it is a seeing with an eye that's not clouded by thought, by intellectualism of a mechanical nature, not distracted by feelings. It requires a watching, a witnessing, of what is. Then the question of "What is search?" will probably be answered. It will be answered by itself.

II Going North

N.Y.U. BACK PREPARES FOR FORDHAM

NEW YORK...BILL SEGAL, N.Y.U.'S SPEEDY LEFT HALFBACK
WHO IS EXPECTED TO PLAY A BIG PART IN THE COMING TILT
WITH FORDHAM, IS PICTURED ABOVE. TOM THORP, HEAD COACH
OF THE VIOLETS, CALLS SEGAL THE SPEEDIEST BACK HE HAS
SEEN IN A DECADE AND PREDICTS A BRILLIANT GRIDIRON FUTURE
FOR THE YOUNG NEW YORK SOPHOMORE.
G-9-27-23-9/00

Youth

Macon, Georgia

My father was a cop. He emigrated from Rumania in the 1890s where he had been an instructor in that army's cavalry. Upon his arrival in the United States, he went to Macon, Georgia, where relatives of my mother's family had previously settled. He was given the job as policeman because in those days local police used horses extensively. He was not particularly fond of life in the South. I recall a story he told. He had been sent by the court to pick up a fugitive accused of murder. In his own words:

"I watched as the court judge, finding the culprit, one named Bud, guilty of murder, cautioned the accused man, 'Bud, this is the third nigger you have killed. Now so help me God, if you kill another one you are going to jail.'"

This was too much for my father, and he decided to leave the South and to settle in the North.

I was born in Macon in 1904. I am unable to give the exact day and month of my birth because my mother never celebrated or kept records of our birthdays. Later when I entered school in Johnstown, Pennsylvania, I did not have any written record to give to the school authorities. When my family communicated with the people in Macon, Georgia, it seems that the birth records were written in ink that faded and there was some confusion about the entries. My mother arbitrarily recalled that I was born on July 17th, 1904. But other evidence indicates that the true birth date was probably June 9th or June 17th. In any event, my mother never made much of a fuss as to exact dates of her children's births, bushing aside questions of exactitude as irrelevancies.

Johnstown, Pennsylvania

I was about nine or ten years old when we moved north to Johnstown in western Pennsylvania. My father was then a traveling salesman, rarely at home, and we children were brought up largely by our mother.

We went to a typical country school. Each child had his own plot of ground to cultivate. I loved gardening, and I loved to see the emergence of the living plants.

Being young, we were forbidden by my mother to go swimming, as children had drowned in the Susquehanna. But I went anyway. It was a great pleasure to swim in the unspoiled rivers. The whole atmosphere of western Pennsylvania was that of an open wilderness. Indians were a familiar presence. All the boys read books about pioneers who traveled West and opened up the country. The decades prior to World War I were a wonderful time for a child.

When World War I started I was all of fourteen years old. I attempted to enlist in the U.S. Air Force. I told them I was eighteen, which was the age at which you could apply as a volunteer in the army. But of course I was pushed aside on the ground that I was too young.

My girl at that time was a certain Virginia Fischer who was a skinny little girl with straight bobbed hair. When we went out picking flowers together she insisted that I give her the flowers. But it had always been my practice to give the flowers to my mother. Virginia tried to persuade me that this was not good behavior, because I, being her boyfriend, was supposed to give the flowers to her. I suppose, like most boys, I was in love with my mother and would bring the flowers to her instead of giving them to Virginia.

There was not much in the way of recreation. The big weekend event may be said to have been the Sunday picnics. I would watch my mother hitch up the buggy. She would place the horse between the shafts and prepare everything. We would have a big lunch basket stowed in the back of the buggy. My mother would mount the carriage, the children would pile in, and off we would go at a nice gallop. This was always an event, each week. My mother would drive about five miles or so out of the town, then she would hitch the horse to a tree. The children would get out and spread the tablecloth and we would have a wonderful lunch. It was a happy time.

I do not recall much about my two older sisters, but I

remember being very close to my younger brother. We always stayed together. We fought against other boys together. My sisters were respectively two and four years older than I was. The age gap made a big difference. When my mother left us alone she always placed my older sister in charge, and my brother and I considered that we were being bullied by the older girls who forced us to do chores we ordinarily did not do.

Life in America in that period was relatively serene. There were few people of very great wealth living around us. There were merchants or entrepreneurs who were, so to speak, very well off. There was an air of certainty that standards of living were getting better and better. It was the period of the advent of the automobile. Money was a scarce commodity, but a dollar bought a great deal. Anyone who wished to work could always get a job. Neighbors helped each other. Local charities provided help for the poor and took care of any poverty pockets that existed. It seemed as if people were not as interested in material things as they are today. People were content with simple pleasures; simple clothing, simple food, simple recreation. There were one or two movie theaters in our neighborhood for which admission was three cents or five cents.

Bronx, New York

In 1914 my father decided to leave Johnstown and bring the family to New York. It seemed there were two main reasons. My sister was getting older and about to marry a young man named Fred Suppes. Fred was the son of a large land proprietor and very well off. But my mother was adamantly opposed to her marrying a Gentile. There were discussions between my mother and father in which she pleaded with him to bring the children where they would meet other Jewish children.

The second reason, and I believe the deciding factor, was that my father was infatuated with the theatre and with what he knew of life in New York, which was to him very glamorous. At any rate, I recall the family taking a four or five hour railway journey to New York

City where my father had rented an apartment in a pleasant neighborhood in the Bronx. Living in the Bronx was like living in the open country. In our backyard we had peach trees, apple and plum trees. There were numerous brooks and streams close by. It was a beautiful time to be a New Yorker. There were no monstrously large apartment houses. The largest structures I recall were only three or four stories high.

Of course, there were some negative factors. Boys from different neighborhoods formed gangs. I was enlisted in a gang which fought with other gangs. There was no use of guns, but there was pretty hard and sharp fighting. Boys from one neighborhood would get together to raid some other territory. Or else there would be an understanding for prearranged meeting in a neutral zone for what we would call a rumble, a fight between two rival groups. We would collect the tops of the ash cans which we used as shields. The two gangs would square off and hurl rocks and sticks at each other. We all accepted this as a way of life. The rumbles usually lasted until the police appeared and broke up the fights.

There were many stables which housed horse-drawn vehicles. As a boy of thirteen or fourteen I had a job as a moving man. I was a strong boy, and I earned a fair amount of money acting as a truck man. One vivid memory I have is of our truck with its two or four horses crossing the newly built Queensborough Bridge. And as we rolled over the bridge near the Queens side there was absolutely nothing but green fields. When I think now of the horrible conglomeration of steel, roads, and buildings that exists today, it is painful. Queens was really filled with Elysian green fields. It is true that there was one factory building at the end of the Queens bridge which was the Chiclet chewing gum factory from which there came a delicious smell of mint. Coney Island was a favorite spot. We would board what was then called an open street car. This open trolley would go bounding across lower Manhattan, then across the Brooklyn Bridge and ride on the rail line to cross Brooklyn. As we approached the ocean, one could smell the delicious sea breeze. For ten cents we were provided with a towel, locker, bathing facilities, and a beautiful stretch of beach. It was great fun to cool off in the ocean. After a wonderful day, we would find a hot dog for five cents and then go for a roller coaster ride.

The principal of our public school was a man named Hugh Smallen. He was a dignified man. He looked like the deacon of a church, very correct in every way. Once he asked me to come to his office where he interrogated me as to my date of birth and middle name, and so on. I had no middle name and felt a little embarrassed about it, so I told him it was Charles. I wondered why he was interrogating me. It seems that I was to be the recipient of the gold Bruckner Medal which was awarded to the brightest student in the borough of the Bronx. I had no idea that I was in any way an outstanding student. I was beginning to be interested in sports and had become the captain of the basketball team and did not pay much attention to my schooling.

We were expected to provide for ourselves at an early age, and I was accustomed to working during the summers. One year, as a bellhop, I earned the large sum of $70 a week through tips at the hotel Martinique, which was tremendous for those times. The Martinique was an elegant hotel with a beautiful bar. If you had a drink, you were served caviar, sturgeon, and smoked salmon for free. I was less than fourteen years old when I applied for the hotel job. They had a pageboy service. When a telephone call came in, someone would go around the lobby shouting in a loud voice, "Call for Mr. Jones, call for Mr. Smith." I was wearing tan shoes at that time. But they needed a boy with black shoes. I said, "Don't worry, I live around here." I didn't. So I dashed out and got myself a five cent shoe shine. "Make them black instead of brown." When I came back, the fellow said, "Oh yes, they're black shoes." That's how I got the job. Later I was promoted from pageboy to bellhop.

The swanky people of New York would come to the Martinique and the McAlpin, which was then a new hotel. I remember bringing something up to one suite, and the woman was Mabel Normand. Mabel Normand was a star and a favorite of Charlie Chaplin. She was a great actress, a beautiful brunette. She said, "I'm going to give you a kiss, besides a dollar." I remember that dollar tip, and a kiss. I was fourteen years old at the time. All the money I made I would give to my mother, and she would return five dollars a week for expenses, which was considerable. Subway fares were five cents. You ate a good meal for fifteen cents.

At sixteen, I became a counselor at a boy's camp. At eighteen I received an athletic scholarship from New York University. I graduated four years later with a Bachelor of Arts degree in business, however, I mainly studied Elizabethan theater.

Airplane view Camp Iroquois, Jaffrey, N.H.

THE SPARTAN

New York, Oct. 31.—When I
Bates, New York University
back, was carried from the field
Syracuse a year ago with a b
mangled leg, his only words to Co
Thorpe were:
"I'm sorry, Tom, I wanted to
this game for you."
Now New York University footb
annals have provided another quo
tion worthy of the Hall of Fame
stitution's roll of honor. William
Siegel, a sophomore from Morr
High School, is a substitute halfba
and flash on his feet. Thorpe, who is
expecting great things from him in
the future, sent him in just before
the close of the first half in Saturday's Rhode Island game to give
him a little actual experience. On
the first play, tackled by two men,
Siegel went down with a broken leg.
The shock and the pain caused Siegel
to let go of the ball. The whistle
ending the half blew at that instant,
and no damage was done, so far as
the fortunes of the game were concerned. But fumbling is a cardinal

Young Basketball Star.

Photo by Pictograms.
Bill Siegel, New York University's

TOM THORP LAUDS SEGAL'S SPIRIT

'Our Team Handicapped," Says Coach in Address Before Heights Students

Tom Thorp, coach of the football
team, lauded the spirit of Bill Siegel,
which is typical of the spirit of the
entire team in struggling against the
handicaps that have faced them
throughout the season, at the meeting
of the Heights Student Organization
on Wednesday, October 31.

"The football team," he said, "has
been handicapped as few other college teams in the country have. The
eligibility rules at N. Y. U. are different from those at many other institutions, notably Fordham, and give
them advantages of which we cannot
avail ourselves. Our lightness as
opposed to the weight of the other
____ is a physical disadvant-

SIEGEL TRYING OUT FOR TRACK TEAM

Popular N. Y. U. Athlete Has Recovered From Football Injury and Wants to Run

HAS IMPRESSIVE RECORD

Bill Siegel is one of the most popular
athletes at New York University. Last
season in a football game with Rhode
Island State College Siegel sustained a
broken leg. His only remark was to the
effect that he was glad it was not the star
back of the team who had been injured in-
fast man, and it is believed that he will
succeed on the cinder path

TOM THORP, N. Y. U.'s genial foot
ball coach and one of the best
known officials and sports authorities
in the land is as mu
York schoolboy.
there is as mu
around New Yo
in the world an
metropolitan sc
equal of any.
Thorp has a
fails to tell, in
York spirit and
in developing f
tion. It deals
popular at the

SIEGEL is a
High Scho
varsity represe

country, socc
ball, captaini
In his freshr
dazzled all s
He is a l
about 135 po
sophomore y
the football
football befo
aptitude and

THE Viole
velop th
in the Colu
pisch. Seig
training, se
utes in so
Two weeks
he was thr
end and h
Thorp ru
with the t
the athlet
Without a
or his disa
"Gee, Ton
wasn't hu
SIR THOM
"And who
Fordham ar
else but. A
up Segal es
and he has
Oh-my-gosh,
soon I wo
if my luck o
Sir Thom
continued to

SIR THOM
and ab
ball affairs
he had ne
was as fast
suit.
"I was saving him." Sir Thor
repeated.

BILL SIEGAL IS INJURED HERO OF THORP'S ELEVEN

By LEONARD COHEN.

When the 1923 football season finally
closes to allow the scriveners and
the fans in general to select the leading figures of the current gridiron year,
New York University will offer one
hero for the season's Hall of Fame.
That man will be William "Bill" Siegal,
at present the hero of the Heights'
campus.

But at this time he looks far from
what one would expect a hero to look
like. For Siegal lies flat ____

Apparently the time Bill spent at New York University left no lasting intellectual impression. He never talked about a professor who was important to him. What remained vivid in his mind were the sports, all the sports in which he excelled. Till the very end of his life he would remember the names of his trainers in the sprint, the javelin, swimming—especially diving—and baseball and football. He would go proudly and easily from one of these sports to another.

Very few people seem to remember their childhood and youth with pleasure. Many people regret what their parents did or didn't do for them. But Bill would remember his happy years in the South and later in New York with joyous nostalgia, smiling happily as he told stories. He was 8 or 9 years old when his family moved to Pennsylvania, and he couldn't understand why the boys at school in Johnstown said, "Willie, repeat 'I ate two-thirds of a custard pie.'" They would roll on the ground laughing at his deep-south Georgian accent. Angry, he returned home and said to his mother, "What's so funny about 'I ate two-thirds of a custard pie?'"

Bill admired his father and adored his mother. He was obviously her favorite. He seldom talked about his parents, and he never painted their portraits. But there is one portrait of his younger brother, Stanley, who was his constant companion, and for whom he had enormous affection. Bill was a really protective older brother. Stanley was a poet.

Bill involved a number of members of his family in his enterprises, including his two daughters. Good father that he was, he always arranged their material life. He always said that a man worthy of the name should be able to provide for at least 20 people.

Stanley died of tuberculosis at the age of 26 and his brother was devastated. Even many years later Bill spoke of his grief with violent emotion. He believed himself guilty of not having watched sufficiently over his brother's health—and he said he would never again allow himself to be taken over by such profound sadness. The family made a kind of cult figure of the young man who died so young. When Bill met the Dalai Lama he remarked that he resembled Stanley. And both his daughters had the same middle name—Stanley

–MBS

Stanley Segal

Marriage to Cora

I like to think that my first sight of Cora was when she was about thirteen years old. I saw her standing on the curbstone in front of her house in the upper Bronx, on Tinton Avenue. She was thirteen, not yet a woman, yet I was struck by her astonishing beauty. I remember thinking "I'm going to marry that girl." I didn't even know who she was. But she stood there with such beauty and intelligence in her expression. She came from a family of four girls. They were of Alsatian descent, all quite beautiful. The older sister was a famous model who appeared very frequently on the cover of *Saturday Evening Post*. She married Louis Nizer, the lawyer. The second sister was a brunette, a flaming beauty. I didn't know my future wife very well. It was rather embarrassing for me to go after her, because she was too young. But as she grew older I kept in touch with her. I first took out the second sister, Rose. She was known as my "girl," though I always had my eye on her younger sister. There was a fourth sister, Nancy, the youngest, about ten years younger than Cora.

Louis Nizer   Mildred Nizer   WCS

Cora Segal

One day, when my family had moved to the Grand Concourse which was then an upper middle class enclave for people living in New York, I called to take out Cora's sister. Cora at that time was about fifteen years old. I remember a little incident. I picked up a book that was lying on the living room table. "Please put that book down. You wouldn't understand it," said Cora. It happened to be Walt Whitman's *Leaves of Grass*. She always thought of me as an athlete. "Oh, well, he's just an athlete." At any rate, when she was about sixteen or seventeen, I would have one of my friends from Yale or Harvard take her out while I took her older sister out. But I always kept my eye on the younger sister. New York was a truly strange and wonderful place. And it was a center for young people coming from Yale, Harvard, and Princeton. We would meet there, go to dances and parties in that great brownstone hotel known as the Waldorf; the old Waldorf Astoria was where the Empire State Building now stands.

The debutantes would give a big party which was open house. All you needed for admission was a dinner jacket and youth. It was the days of prohibition, too. There was a good deal of drinking and young people getting sick on bad liquor. People made their own gin at home. The illicit liquor was like the drugs of our time.

I was married about 1930. I was twenty-six or twenty-seven. And she was about nineteen, and already a schoolteacher. One did not need a college degree, then, but took special courses in a teacher's training school.

Professional Life

1 Make do with what you have.
2 Stay with it.
3 Do only what is necessary.
4 Take your time. –WCS

New York, New York– Beginning of Professional Life

By that time I had graduated from college. I had had one or two jobs on Wall Street. Then I worked for Macy's as a trainee. Executives-in-training had to wear a starched collar and necktie. I said to myself, "That's not for me." I left Macy's and got a job as a proofreader for a plastics magazine, Hoffman Publications. But after a few weeks I asked about giving me something else to do. I went out selling advertising space and subscriptions. I sold so much it was astonishing. I would come back with many orders. I could see the pleasure of the publishers. After a while I was given the job of running of one of their magazines. It was a men's fashion magazine, an associated trade paper. I decided I was going to get married, went to the publisher and requested a five-dollar raise. He said, "Five dollars! I'll give you three dollars a week." I left him to start my own publication, *The Reporter*.

WILLIAM C. SEGAL
Editor and Publisher

CORA JOAN MANTEL
Circulation Manager
. . . and general inspiration
of the staff is this charming
young lady. She receives
more lunch invitations from
bigwigs in the industry than
Greta Garbo. Chief ambition
is to raise Reporter's circulation to one million paid
subscriptions.

S. C. STANLEY
Managing Editor
M. E. Stanley managed to
acquire a bachelor of law
degree and a valuable background of economics before
hitching up with the Reporter.

Family staff

Trips to Europe, Meeting Pijoan – First Mentor

Each summer there was a mass exodus of teachers to Europe. They were the ones who traveled, who took vacations. We went to Europe at least once every year. Our routine was to go to Paris by boat. From Paris we would travel to Italy, Spain, Switzerland, Germany, wherever we wished.

We made one trip with Mildred, Cora's older sister. Each of us had bought a round trip to Russia, all expenses included, I think it was $160. It must have been around 1930, '31. We went to Russia on a cruise sponsored by the French Line. And the French Line became the synonym of the milk cow for us.

We rented a little apartment in a hotel in the middle of Paris. It was extremely cheap. Two or three dollars a day with meals. On one or two trips I was accompanied by my brother, who had just finished law school. Almost immediately, he would make friends with some French girl—usually one with an automobile. So our transportation was well taken care of as long as he was in Paris. Paris was the focus of our vacation periods. We loved that city. Perhaps people will remember the song, "The Last Time I Saw Paris." It was that way for many Americans. I remember being overwhelmed by the beauty and the "chic," and the openness of the city during the 30s. The girls seemed more beautiful than the American girls. One could not help being attracted to them.

One European trip we met Jose Pijoan, a well-known Spanish art critic and an important influence in our lives. We met in the early '30s. We were sun-decking, Cora and I, when suddenly this big, elegant, white-haired man appeared and began to speak. We were very young, about 25 or 26 and he must have been in his 50s, old for us. He began to speak about art. We didn't know much about him, except that he was a professor of art at the University of Chicago. We began dinning with him and his wife, Theresa. Pijoan was one of the Barcelona radicals in the art and intellectual movement. Theresa came from an aristocratic Spanish family and there was a great scandal because, being a Catholic in a Catholic country, Pijoan had divorced his wife and she had divorced her husband so that they could be together and marry.

Later, my association with Pijoan in the U.S. deepened. He knew Frank Lloyd Wright. He knew Orozco. He insisted that I should become a student of Orozco. I went with him to Florence, to study frescos. Pijoan was a great art dealer on the side, although he was head of the Chicago Art Institute. He was always wheeling and dealing in art. He asked me to retouch an El Greco hand, which I did, quite expertly, because by that time I was a good painter. Then, in Geneva he would take me with him: he would go to enjoy or evaluate old masterpieces. He was always concerned whether a thing was genuine or fake.

We kept up our acquaintance in New York where we had this wonderful visit with Orozco. We were in a night club. New York was in a depression. There was no money around. Orozco was in New York and once I had a due-bill from advertising which entitled us to spend money at the Hollywood restaurant on 48th and Broadway. It was a famous café and was probably run by gangsters. One evening was marvelous. We were there with Orozco and Cora, Pijoan and myself. Pijoan brought out of his pocket a Tanagra and asked Orozco and me how we liked it. While the naked girls were right behind us, we were examining a Tanagra figure.

I remember one night when we were talking about revolution, someone said, "Well, Orozco, you painted the great revolutionary frescos. They all have to be social, tell the story." He held out his thumb and his forefinger and said, "Look, a little etching, just the size of a postage stamp, that Rembrandt made is more revolutionary than all of the big frescos that Rivera and I are making."

Pijoan arranged for Orozco to paint the Pomona fresco in the college, which is still there. He used to say: "Can you imagine these square Christians, out there, who ran the college, and they had this big Prometheus with his big penis sticking out. What must they have thought that I got Orozco to paint this. But here it is, the glory of Pomona to this day." He was proud that he could get commissions for Orozco.

He did some of his work in Chester. He would spend a couple of weekends and I was fascinated at the way he would write his three-volume history of art, which was published all over the world. He would sit down with a stack of photographs, and then we would write from the photographs. He would finish a 600-page book in a couple of weeks.

Starbuck and WCS

The World's Fair -1939

My associate, Starbuck, was a promoter. He and I were supposed to put up a major building at the World's Fair. That was really the heyday of my career. By that time I was established as a publisher. Burt Bachrack was running the magazine. Starbuck and I would go around and sell space for a new building in the World's Fair. We put up the building. That's what broke us. We spent too much on construction and lost money. Each company had to put up its own building. Costs were higher than we anticipated. But, most importantly, I made the mistake of making the building too big.

Reporter Staff – 1938

American Fabrics 1946–1980

With the success of the different trade publications that followed *The Reporter*, life became boring for me. I decided in 1946 to publish a magazine that was strictly my idea of a fine magazine. It took approximately a hundred thousand dollars, which at that time was a large sum. I spent two months at the seashore putting together this publication. I later devoted a good deal of time, energy and money to its production. The result was *American Fabrics*. I figured that such a magazine would

Burt Bachrack and WCS

41

at least have an artistic life, and would intrigue a number of people. Much to my astonishment, the magazine took off almost immediately. There evidently was a market for a quality publication. The textile and allied chemical fibers, clothes, and fashion industries needed a truly representative and beautiful publication, which *American Fabrics* undoubtedly was. The magazine continued to prosper from the first day it was published, although there were some difficult periods. It served as a flagship for the group of ordinary or less ordinary trade publications.

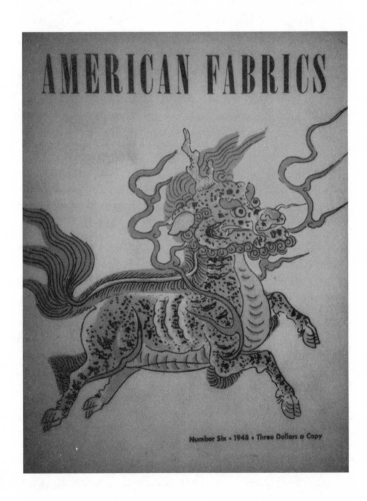

Gentry 1951-57

After a while I became more ambitious and decided that inasmuch as the world of publication at that time had acknowledged *American Fabrics*, why not come out with similar publications for the consumer fields? I decided to publish a magazine called *Gentry*. The idea was to have a very top publication. I mean that in the sense that the production, the printing, and the paper would all be first rate. I would also employ the idea of tip-ins and swatches which had seemed to strike the fancy of the *American Fabrics* readers. *Gentry* was a phenomenal success in one sense, in that it received reams of publicity. It truly had a superior audience. We ran ads, full-page ads, in the *New Yorker*, *Time* magazine and *The New York Times*. These ads brought in a great deal of subscription money for the first six months of publication and pre-publication. Thus, we let our guard down, thinking we were a sure success. The circulation kept going up . . . the price of the magazine was two dollars a copy.

The response was wonderful. So, we went on and on. But the magazine was much more costly to produce than I had anticipated. While we had a great deal of advertising, we did not price each page sufficiently. At one time the editor of *Playboy* came to visit me and proposed an alliance, or an exchange of stock. But at that time, *Playboy* was considered too far out, so we lost a great opportunity, at least to be independently wealthy as publishers.

Gentry was the albatross that sank our ship. I kept putting more and more of the money we made on *American Fabrics* and other publications into *Gentry*. I suppose it fed my vanity. It was considered innovative and creative and it was a consumer magazine. When I heard the death knell of *Gentry*, I arranged to go on a trip to Japan. On this trip, I was approached by a large industrialist to become a consultant to his firm, a Japanese conglomerate. That was the beginning of my long association with Japan.

Publisher of 11 Magazines

Frank Lloyd Wright's disciple, Alvin Lustig, was the most avant-garde designer of the forties. Bill used his services in a number of ways. Lustig designed the entire office, furniture, lighting, carpets and art objects. A long article in the magazine Interiors *showed the office under the title "By Unorthodox Design," subtitled "Headquarters for Publishing Firm." Lustig also designed Segal's Park Avenue apartment, equal in elegance, which was also featured in many articles.*

Bill didn't always agree with Lustig's minimalist design, but still he made him art director of this enterprise and allowed him to design the first cover for Gentry *which was the head of a Greek sculpture.*

It is interesting to analyze this first issue of Gentry *because it proves the extent to which Bill was its ever-present author, at a time when no similarly artistic publication existed in the United States. First of all, the elegant advertisements were all in the front of the magazine, so that the following articles could be read without interruption. The table of contents had a particular layout, with a mini-illustration for each article. All of Bill's life and interests were in that first issue: a riding lesson, built around his daughter Margaret; a page of music by Thomas de Hartmann, who arranged Gurdjieff's music; several pages on how to build a sauna, based on his own sauna in Chester; two pages devoted to twenty of Rembrandt's self-portraits; the first publication in America of* Siddharta *by Hermann Hesse. Already there was Bill's interest in Buddhism: "He strove in vain to dispel the conception of time, to imagine Nirvana and Samsara as one." an idea that pleased Bill immensely. Finally, there was a section called "Gentry Fashion," addressed to men as elegant as the editor. Attached to the sophisticated photographs were samples of cloth hand-pasted to each page. These hand-pasted samples were characteristic of Bill's magazines, and of course they cost a fortune to produce. The quality of the text, of the photography, and of the paper was excellent.*

When I asked him why he chose the Empire State Building for his office, Bill answered:

"It was a prestigious building, and well located. Besides, I received a good offer from the proprietor, whom I knew. A school boy friend, Helmsley-Spear, who had taken over the building became the partner of this friend of mine. One day I was riding up the elevator with the two proprietors. My friend said, 'Bill, I'm following what you have been doing with *Gentry*. You are not going to make any money out of this magazine business. Come and see me.' He became a very rich man, endowed stadiums and colleges. But I never went up to see him."

—MBS

WCS publishing headquarters designed by Alvin Lustig, Empire State Building, 1946

Alvin Lustig's pioneering design of open office space

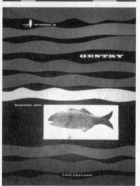

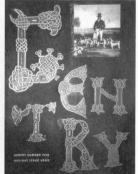

Letters from Jose Pijoan

3 July 1953

Dear Bill and Cora,

Our last letter was rather serious because we asked you to consider the need of making Gentry more intellectually minded. We are afraid that in the near future, you will be a little disappointed of having served to develop the vanity of so many swanky wearers of checker-board jackets! Of course those are the ones that we want to fish and to turn into complete human beings, not only mannequins of windows of Saks Fifth Avenue. We want to make them conscious of the possibilities for thinking and enjoying abundant life.

We realize that Gentry started with the patronage of that kind of people and we have to coax and flatter them. Dress is also an important part of the endeavor of mankind and we don't complain that you teach those nice looking people to drink good wines and travel around the world with a complete wardrobe, but at the same time we have to put in their hands spiritual food and noble wine and for this we want to serve Gentry and its masters, Bill and Cora.

But for the sake of both Gentry and its masters, we have been preaching reform and you have paid attention only in part to this voice. What seems to us necessary in the U.S. is something between the magazine of daily information like Life and Collier's and the stuffy high-brow Atlantic Monthly, Harper's etc. An Atlantic Monthly in attractive style with illustrations and pages that have the appeal of Gentry is what in our understanding you ought to do. Gentry up to the present is only an experiment for you to learn. After all you come not from the dust, but not from the laboratories and institutions of research. Your very ignorance is precious.

29 July 1953

What we learned in your letter is that Gentry is not self-supporting and you have to earn to keep up this creature which is devouring your own with a remote hope of making a fortune with it. We shall try to clear these points in this letter which will be long. For this reason you are asked to read it at home and have patience, because we may miss the points for excess of love. We are both excessive, not equanimous and balanced.

Now about Gentry. You started Gentry and even if it were a mistake you are bound to carry your load to the whole consequences. You are necessary to Gentry just because you are dissatisfied with actual and material life. This very ambition of permanency, stability and inner growth will give to the magazine a character that is to make it important and different from all the rest. The Reader's Digest attempts to popularize trends of thought and action in a general way, but it is essentially intellectual what the Reader's D. communicates. It is good to be posted even if it is distributed in the style low and monotonous of the factory at Pleasantville.

Our readers or lookers are these very men that wear jackets in American fabrics by Saks. The lady Treanor of Los Angeles who says to us, Gentry is on my glass table in the living room; the wife of a lawyer at Tulsa post grad of Chicago who finds in Gentry an inspiration to live in Oklahoma, and others of the same kind . . . Our aim is to raise the level of the high brows and high ups, potentates, captains of industry, Wall street men to step higher. Do you remember the article "The education of soul, not your mind," in Gentry. You are realizing a national service.

We also felt that Gentry ought to reduce the fashion pictures and not to be exclusively a man's journal. For this we proposed articles on admirable ladies: The scientist who discovered vaccination in the Turkish harems, the one who imported quinine, another who made the first artery operations . . . beside Isabelle d'Este, "la Prima Dona del Mondo," and many others.

You have done such tremendous effort, and a successful one, you created a type of magazine entirely new. We think that with the show you made during those three years, you are entitled to recognition and you will get it.

America, bad or good, is the only hope of the world. You are helping this poor human race to come out of the mire.

If you don't succeed in carrying out your plans, you learned so much about the way of making publications that working for other people you ought to make your fortune. This is America, not the America that we dreamt of and for which we published Gentry. America is now the imperator which controls financially and politically the whole world. We wanted with Gentry to contribute to make her the leader in arts and science. Do not be insulted, but my slogan was to make a real homo sapiens of the homo americanus.

Jose Pijoan

Comments from Colleagues

This is the man who still dresses conservatively in custom-tailored, navy-blue, double breasted suits, still wears Charvet shirts and ties, still treasures an ancient felt hat from Lock of St. James Street, which he originally shaped to his head by wearing it in the shower.

That is the Bill Segal I have always admired, a man who values the work done, not the pay received; a man for whom the satisfaction comes from work done well. And that, perhaps, is why he has never built a publishing empire like other men whose primary goal is money and power. For Bill, the challenge and the achievement came from work he could do himself, not from hiring others to do it.

I must say something about the quality of that work which he did so quickly and with such seeming ease. Once, I spent a long evening writing an important editorial which he wanted to publish in *American Fabrics*. It was an editorial which took a policy position the publisher would be required to support, so I was a little nervous about it. In the morning I came into the office and handed him three sheets of double-spaced typing, saying, "Bill, I've written a piece which I'd like you to read." He took the pages, flipped through them quickly and handed them back to me in about thirty seconds. "Fine," he said. "Run it!" I was outraged. "But you didn't read it," I cried. "I spent a long time on this piece and I think you ought to read it carefully." "But I did," he said. "Then tell me what it says," I challenged. And he did. With all points covered. And we ran the editorial. So we never wasted time on conferences. There was no chain of command. No delayed decisions.

—Cecil Lubell

American Fabrics made a rather serious sensation in the magazine world both for its economics and aesthetics. No one before had ever published an industrial magazine on such good stock with such sophisticated art work. Nor had they ever covered an industry so thoroughly with respect for its potential, its history and its arts. There was a sort of collective gasp of surprise and wonder. Could it survive? Perhaps out of curiosity, perhaps it was so obviously useful, circulation soon zoomed to twelve thousand. And there it stayed for better than thirty years. In the magazine market that is glorious survival.

—Robert Riley

It was 1976, and I had created an interesting red, white and blue abstract flag cover, a kind of American bicentennial graphic. I thought it looked terrific. I called a meeting in the conference room to show it to you. I presented the cover. I waited for your comments, your approval. You said nothing. For a long time, we both stared at the cover. Silence. Was it good, bad? More silence. Then you slowly reached out and took the cover into your hands and very slowly, tore it in half, from top to bottom. I can still hear the sound of that thick card stock being torn, deliberately, slowly. I was shocked. You held the two halves of my cover in each hand and looked at me. Then you laid them on the table and slid the two halves almost together, leaving about one eighth inch of the white ragged torn edges showing between the two halves, making a subtle collage. "I like your cover, it's really good," you said. "Always leave a trace of the hand in your work."

—Adrian Butash

Segal lived a remarkable parallel existence apart from his publishing life, which further informed *Gentry*'s content beyond the conventions of men's fashion. As a follower and confidante of G.I. Gurdjieff, the Armenian-born mystic who led an esoteric movement aimed at joining the wisdom of the East with the vitality of the West, Segal devoted much of his time and energy to raising the spiritual level of everyday existence. He used *American Fabrics* and *Gentry*, in part, as outlets for personal exploration that he felt could help others cope with their lives. Segal practiced Buddhism and sought out themes for magazine articles that delved deeper into human experience than was typical of the fare usually found in fashion publications.

But Segal was also a pragmatic businessman who found ways to align his humanistic, artistic pursuits within the constraints of trade publishing. "When we launched *Gentry*," He said, in an interview shortly before his death, "we visualized it as a magazine that could have a great cultural influence. At that time in the U.S., we were largely a nation of hicks. There was no culture. People did not know how to dress well, how to eat well, how to order wine or what to read. They were unfamiliar with the world of art. We thought we could have a civilizing influence through this publication." His practical goal was "to allow people to see the aesthetic element that was a factor in choosing clothing. The importance of Gentry was to make the clothing a part of the fine art of living."

Thus, he bolstered features on menswear of the day with articles on a host of other subjects—art, history, philosophy, travel—as well as with short fiction pieces by leading authors. One thing seems certain: If Segal started *Gentry* today, he would be celebrated for his independence—and the buzz on *Gentry* would be deafening.

—Steven Heller

Conversation on Painting

(transcript)

Q. ARE there any SPECIAL WRITINGS YOU WOULD RECOMMEND FOR YOUNG ARTISTS?

W.S. I have been helped ~~very~~ greatly by reading Delacroix. ~~For example~~ he clarified MANY thing~~s~~ THAT WERE NOT clear TO ME. In going over ~~my~~ SOME old paintings I SAW TOO MUCH preoccupation with details. ~~The~~ The more I tried to refine, the more I slipped into the "please the critic" mode of painting. Delacroix WRITES ON THIS. HE ALSO POINTS OUT THAT IT IS NECESSARY to paint with thought ~~and~~ Thought HELPS TO SAY what you want to say, AND RESULT~~s~~ IN freedom from ~~the~~ small details which OFTEN CLOUD THE PAINTERS LARGER VISION. ONE MORE naturally move~~s~~ TOWARDS A WIDER TOWARDS A BROADER ~~view,~~ way of painting, — without ~~losing the nuances,~~ FRESHNESS AND ~~which~~ BRING joy ~~into~~ to the viewer~~s~~ Delacroix ~~is~~ IS ALWAYS helpful. I wish I had read him when I was young.

He also elaborates on the struggle between ~~emphasizing~~ the drawing, OR ANOTHER and the ~~fascination of using~~ color, of letting one ~~predominate~~. I never had that difficulty, but I was stuck for a number of years in the drawing mode, ~~neglecting to see the potential~~s of ~~the~~ color~~s~~.

Q. CAN YOU SAY MORE ABOUT "THE BROAD APPROACH"?

W.S. An ~~appropriate~~ example ~~~~ is Gauguin's painting ~~of~~ "The Siesta," ~~which he made,~~ in the TAHITI Islands. When you look at this picture, you see, ~~~~ that the hat is ~~so~~ broadly rendered, — PAINTED SWIFTLY, YET EASILY the same with other ~~~~ details in the picture. THERE IS just a blob of bright orange for the dress ~~~~. Speaking about the hat, ~~~~ simply because it is considered ~~an~~ inconsequential ~~detail~~ in relation to THE ~~a~~ face, ~~for~~ ~~example,~~ ~~painters~~ ERS FREQUENTLY FEEL FREE TO RENDER ~~Brush~~ THIS ACCESSORY — AND OTHER DETAILS

III meeting P.D. Ouspensky

Watercolor, 4 East 9th Street, NYC

58

Meeting P.D. Ouspensky

Life at Franklin Farms

*"Parceque c'etait lui,
Parceque c'etait moi"* –Montaigne

I was in the middle period of my business career. We had just moved into larger quarters in the Empire State Building and we were adding publications almost every four months, or so it seemed. I had arrived at a point in my life when things were going along very well, financially speaking. The magazines I had started were successful. I had a good staff of people working with me. This was the beginning of 1940. At that particular period I was in a position of being independent, financially. I had made a lot of money in publications, and lost much of it in my investments in the World's Fair. At any rate, life was beginning to be rather boring. In 1941 the war was imminent. Shortages of materials appeared. People began to demand services, and industrial activity increased at a very strong pace. No matter where you turned, there was a demand for your services or products. It was my daily practice to walk up Fifth Avenue from my house at Ninth Street in the Village to the Empire State Building. One day I spied an old acquaintance of mine crossing the street. We got together, and began to speak. His name was Theo Fruchsman, and he was connected with the technical services of the U.S. Navy. He said, "Bill, you don't look like your old self. You seem to be a little heavier. Why don't you try some exercise." I answered, "You know I've had enough exercise in my time. That's not my cup of tea." Then he suggested, "Why not try some yoga." Hatha yoga was beginning to be popular. His suggestion stuck in my mind. Later on I met someone who conducted a class in yoga. I became interested and quite adept in this, let's call it exercise. I never viewed yoga as anything except physical exercise.

I would take my family to Fire Island each summer. One day we were invited to a party given by a Madame Ganna Walska who was an opera star. At the party some-

P.D. Ouspensky

Madame Ouspensky

59

one mentioned that there was a man named P.D. Ouspensky, who had just come over from England and who was giving lectures on esoteric subjects. My wife and I were invited to attend one of his lectures, and to meet him at his country place in New Jersey. This was Franklin Farms in Mendham, New Jersey. Franklin Farms had been the mansion of a former governor of New Jersey. It was a beautiful place. We accepted. It was a formal dinner. There was an assemblage of about thirty distinguished people.

At this occasion I met Madame Ouspensky. The evening was quite unusual. The people who served us were obviously from the upper social classes, not ordinary servants but people who were followers of Ouspensky. They did the cooking, serving, waiting, washing up. This was, I suppose, one of the first New Age circles in America. Mr. Ouspensky was an impressive man. He spoke with an authority, which could not help but make a strong impact on me. So, I said I would like to go to his lectures, which I understood were going to be held in New York each week. That is how I made contact with Mr. Ouspensky. I started to go to his lectures.

There would be an average of thirty-five people in each one of these weekly lectures which were wonderful because he didn't broach anything that was of a low quality or a low nature. He wouldn't permit any question unless it made sense. He was very near-sighted and held a book close to his eyes. Someone would ask a question, he would say, "Who said that?" Someone asked another question, "Next" . . . "No good." He dismissed them just like that. You had to be on your toes and you had to formulate a real question before you would get an answer.

Some subjects aroused a great deal of interest on the part of Mr. Ouspensky. Time and relationship between different universes. I would ask a question about time, and then he would go off . . . "Time is the unique subjective." He then worked out his table of time and different cosmos. He was always interested in dimensions of time. His theory was "We don't see reality, because of inability to enter into the time of another creature, another universe." He did not have a formatory mind, he questioned everything.

After a few weeks of lectures we were invited to come to the farm on a regular basis. We went as weekend working members. My wife, Cora, didn't want to go out there. But after a few weeks, as I began to narrate what I had heard from Mr. Ouspensky, she too became interested.

We were spending each weekend at Franklin Farms. In the summertime I recall getting up as early as four o'clock in the morning to take the boat from Fire Island to Bay Shore. This I accepted as a privilege. I was happy to be able to do this. There was a dedication. The war had broken out. Gasoline was rationed, and it was difficult to own a car, to get gasoline. But it was a wonderful period in many ways. We spent weekends and sometimes week-long periods at Franklin Farms. It was a haven of peace, quiet and it gave us a devotional solitude which I had not experienced in my life before. My wife was more interested than I was in spiritual things. She could see the drift that was taking place in me towards a life-driven existence. Finding a system through Ouspensky's lectures was a god-send to me.

Chester – "This is the place."

Franklin Farms was wonderful at that period because very few people came. We were in the midst of the war. Labor was very difficult to come by. One had to know one's way around to have meat, and fresh food. Everything was directed towards the war effort. By that time several of my staff had become officers in the armed forces. I was invited to come to Washington where I was offered a colonelship in the army. It was agreed that I would start in the aviation branch of the service. But I was never called up. At any rate, the war effort went on, while our own esoteric search continued. We had the chance to speak quite often with Mr. Ouspensky. The days at the farm were wonderful. So peaceful and filled with good efforts, with a really intense search for oneself, with good discipline. I benefited from the strong physical tasks. I was in charge of the woods. Every weekend when people came from out of town, I would be assigned six or seven people who would work with me. We were out in the woods, lifting heavy logs and carrying them. Ouspensky said that when you do this very heavy work, you breathe differently and the breathing regulates your insides, your guts, so you're sexually better off with women than you would be if you didn't do this work.

Ouspensky's office was at Franklin Farms. I had a lot of time and would go to visit him in the middle of the afternoon when nobody was there. We would talk. I remember Mrs. Howarth would come in, she was the head of "the movements" and she would say, "Mr. Segal has to come with us and do movements." Ouspensky, instead of saying, "Go ahead," would (growling) say to me, "Sit down. What are you bothering with movements for?"

I decided I would not go to the seashore because I would rather spend summers near Mr. Ouspensky. We looked around for a place not far from Franklin Farms. One day, passing a place with an interesting waterfall in Chester New Jersey, I immediately said, "this is the place" without even looking at the house. We bought Chester with its thirty acres of woods and a nice little house. The children were going to camp each summer, so we spent summers at Chester, or at the farm. What was especially striking at Franklin Farms during this period was the arrival of many visitors from England. There were a number of the Ouspensky followers who were also strongly entrenched in the British Secret Service. There were a series of two or three day visits from young Englishmen who would spend some time there, and then disappear, frequently to return. I got to know a number of them, and was always impressed with the dedication and the intelligence of these patriotic Englishmen, all involved in the war against Hitler.

Ouspensky did not have an American way of life. He had Oxford dons at his disposal. He had a wine cellar. Every Sunday night we would have a formal dinner. We were farming people, and would dress up in black dinner jackets. I was being served by an English lord. On one hot day, while working in the fields, a man took off his shirt and there was a crest embroidered on his under-wear. Later on I found out that the man I was calling, "Hey, Pentland," was a Lord Pentland. Bissing had inherited half of Cyprus. I would work in the fields or the stalls, in the manure heap, and I'd come home and find that all of Bissing's shoes, including his working shoes, were made by Lobb. Lord Ramsbottom became the head of a big Buddhist monastery in India.

The routine at Franklin Farms was always more or less the same. A few of the older people would make up the day's list and form teams. Usually the men's work was done by a team of about seven men. The women's work was the same. The day began with a short period of silence. In the middle of the morning we had a coffee break, always an occasion for a brief exchange. Lunch took place in the large dining room. There was very little speaking at lunch. We ate at long tables. People took pride in cleaning up quickly and efficiently. In the after-noon we followed the same work routine as in the morn-ing. Usually the day ended with coffee or tea and a read-ing which was given to us by Madame Ouspensky. The readers were the older men, including Rodney Collin Smith, who was a favorite disciple of Mr. Ouspensky.

Working at Franklin Farms

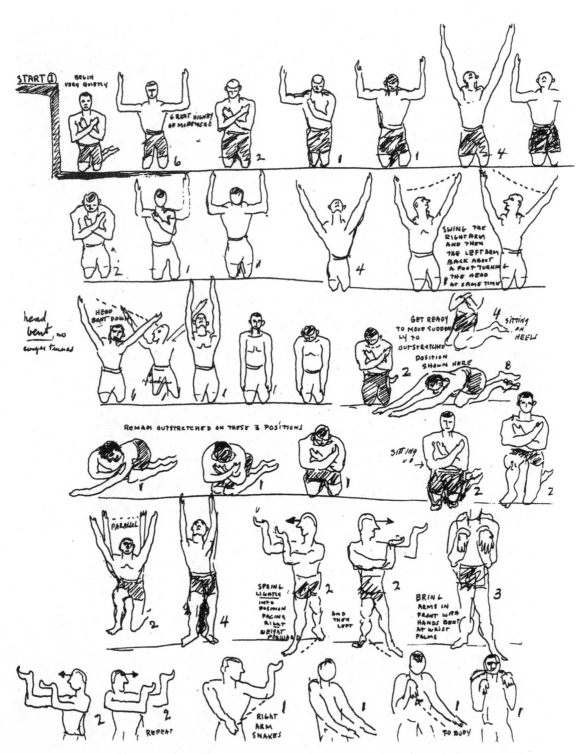

Part of the movement, "La grande prière" – sketch by WCS

64

Activities at the farm were most varied. For example, one of the men was an expert at splicing fruit trees together. This was Martin Benson, who was able to make grafts from one fruit tree to another. I cut a great deal of wood, because it was needed to keep Madame Ouspensky's bedroom warm. The fire went continuously day and night. Summer and winter her fire was kept going.

Then there was the raising of the crops. Chickens were kept to provide the eggs. Much of the produce, especially during the war, was sold to neighboring produce merchants. In fact, much of our income for the running of the farm came from the sale of the vegetables, chickens and eggs. There was always the question of the upkeep of this large three hundred acre farm and its buildings. The staff who lived there, mostly women, were always happy when the weekends arrived, because then they received a great deal of help. Quite a big staff was needed to run the farm. The weekend people provided the necessary help. One day during a snowstorm, when no taxis were available, we were driving and came across Mrs. Dione Lucas carrying a load of meat on her shoulder. I said, "What are you doing?" "Madame Ouspensky needs meat. I am carrying meat to the farm," she answered. Mrs. Lucas was the founder of the Cordon Bleu in New York, quite a distinguished character. She trudged along with the meat on her shoulder. It was quite an eye opener.

In New York, we used to meet Mr. Ouspensky at Longchamps, on Madison Avenue, which stayed open all night. After the meeting, which ended at about ten o'clock, we would go to this Longchamps and have supper. There were no women with us. There was Wolton, Collin Smith, Holmes, myself and Forman, four or five men. Ouspensky would start to drink (his favorite drink was apricot brandy) and we stayed until three or four in the morning.

When I asked Bill about his friendship with Ouspensky, he said, "I liked him and he liked me," adding, in French, *"Parceque c'etait lui, Parceque c'etait moi."* But perhaps as important to him as the ideas displayed at Mendham was all the wood he chopped to warm Mme. Ouspensky's room.

Ouspensky was Bill's first spiritual master, and for the rest of his life Bill had an affectionate admiration for this superior spirit who opened doors of perception to hitherto unknown places. But Bill was too occupied with his professional life at that time to really pursue the ideas of his Russian teacher. Ouspensky, on his side, apparently, completely shared Bill's feelings of deep friendship.

The daily life of Franklin Farms, the combination of physical exercise and spiritual concerns appealed to Bill in a way that just intellectual activities would never have done. It was there that Bill developed his passion for wood-working. The various farm activities pleased Bill. His friend James George tells of an incident made to create a close relationship:

"The moment with Bill was not at all ordinary and I still feel the shock of it as I write. Bill and I were cutting tall grass with scythes on a hill behind the main house at Franklin Farms one sunny summer day. The heat was intense and the air was heavy. I grew impatient with the task, wanting to get it done and over with, scything with more haste than attention. Suddenly I saw that my big scythe had nearly eviscerated Bill who was working facing me on the slope below. Had he not been fully aware of the proximity and danger, he could not have instantly pulled back from my blind swing of the blade which narrowly missed him. The next moment was unforgettable. No recriminations, no negative reaction from Bill. In fact no words were exchanged—just a silent awakening to what had happened, and a wordless bonding between us. His presence in that moment of my sleep remains with me today. The presence of a Japanese samurai who had just dodged his enemy's sword."

The arrival of Gurdjieff at Mendham, after Ouspensky's death, seems to have changed Bill's idea of a spiritual master. The presence of this new master, the teacher of his teacher, had an immediate, unexpected and enormously strong effect—stronger than any other. Often, more than a half century *later, when he was over ninety, Bill would say, "I wonder how I would feel now if I had just met Mr. Gurdjieff for the first time."*

G.I. Gurdjieff

Spiritual Masters: Linking Heaven and Earth

A Conversation with Marvin Barrett

MB: What are the signs of a spiritual master?

WCS: One could begin by examining the qualities one would wish to find in a master. Is he intelligent? Does he possess common sense? Compassion? Is he independent? Courageous? Capable? Can he convey the teachings in a way that speaks directly to the student? Is he in control? One might also expect many of these qualities in a student.

MB: What is the difference between personal contact with a master and contact through writing?

WCS: The aim of the master is to link heaven and earth. Contact with a master is a definite physical event where energy is transferred between two people. From that point of view, a direct relationship is vital. That happens very rarely. But a group of people can utilize one master's time very well. Maybe a master can't devote all his attention to a single individual, but a lit-

WCS and Marvin Barrett

tle cloister around him can serve as a stimulation for others. Even a modicum of relationship with a master gives rise to an openness and a reception of energies which is not possible without the teacher's presence. The question is, is the ultimate master inside you? It may be that the ultimate master arises at the moment that I'm still and I recognize this ever abiding presence which has nothing to do with me as I generally conceive of myself.

MB: What is the relationship between the exterior master and the interior master that you're describing? Does the outer activate the inner?

WCS: There is a relationship between the exterior and the interior. My stillness has its effect on you. So does the wind. In a sense, we are called to live between two worlds—between the objective and subjective worlds. It is possible to encompass all the richness of impressions that are offered by nature and at the same time remain in contact with one's subjective "I." I can sit here with all my fantasies and dreams, but if I can't be still for a moment and stop the movements that generally go on, I cannot partake of certain vibrations which are always present. It comes to include people in the deepest sense, and we begin to know what we cannot know with our ordinary limitations—the voice of God.

MB: Is the master someone intervening between you and God?

WCS: Not in the strict sense. It's only when an opening to the intrusion of another force appears that the recognition of what might be called God is possible. But it has nothing to do with whether a master acts or not.

MB: In the Zen tradition, the master is the one who instruments your illumination.

WCS: It seems that the master is there to help clear the way. While one lusts for food or sex and is beset by such thoughts, nothing is possible. So the master challenges the disciple, sometimes quite harshly, until he is willing

to give up those attachments. A master carries the responsibility of refining the capacities of the disciple so that he can begin to realize his true nature.

MB: Are there two functions of the master—one of teaching and the other of example? Is the example of the master a form of teaching?

WCS: There are many ways of imparting a teaching. When I was in Paris with Gurdjieff, two or three of the oldest men used to go to the Turkish baths with him weekly. Once when we finished our bath, I remember seeing him walking ahead naked. And I realized that he was teaching something I never could learn by talk.

There's also the time I went to pay my respects to Kobori Roshi's widow in Kyoto, shortly after he died in 1991. He was a great aristocrat. One of his ancestors invented the tea ceremony. Another was the architect who designed most of the famous seventeenth century temple gardens. At the time of our visit, Kobori's appointed successor had taken his place. He was only about forty-five or fifty at the time. Being older than this new man, I looked him over. He was a stocky peasant type, unlike the tall, aristocratic Kobori. At one point I asked him, what makes you think you can fill the master's shoes? He looked me in the eye and said, "You'll know I can succeed him when I can impart the teachings with my back." With that he swung around and walked from the room. I had the distinct feeling that he was able to do just that—teach with his back. I felt the same way about Gurdjieff, that he was imparting teaching just as he was.

MB: Certainly the spine is very important in many religious traditions. There is also the concept of those in other fields becoming so masterful that they really become masters in spirituality. For instance, the singer Marian Anderson, whom I met briefly, was a consummate artist who had no ego. She had a presence that conceivably grew out of her mastery of the art of singing. Of course, it may have been something that was there from the beginning. But that is an example of someone in the arts who has developed this quality.

WCS: It's a question of levels. In the teaching of art or music, the master passes on a very high level of technique together with the ability to sustain an effort. Even an athlete receives this kind of training. It's a question of holding the student's attention. Certainly a strong teacher can really give you the works.

MB: Or hit you in your ego.

WCS: I would say D.T. Suzuki was a master. He consciously and very nobly undertook to educate a dull American. He gave me what he could. Gurdjieff, of course, was too big to teach you directly. You had to watch him. So I watched.

MB: You had to extract it from him.

Mme. de Salzmann and Dr. Suzuki, Kita Kamakura, 1966

WCS: Yes. And I saw it, as I said, in the way he walked, the way he handled people, the way he helped them. He kept his cool, as it were. And so we learned. We learn from the bad things as well as the good things. We're continually learning, whether we know it or not. There's a constant input of impressions, knowledge, and energies received in your head, your stomach, your hands, that is present even in the feel of a cup of tea. It goes on every moment of the day. But we're too small. We can't grasp it. Shakespeare put it very well: What fools these mortals be.

MB: Blake said if a fool persists in his folly he will become wise. Everything has meaning, if you observe in the proper way. It's there to teach you.

WCS: That doesn't disprove the first part at all.

MB: But it gives you hope.

WCS: One has to be intelligent enough to analyze it. Otherwise we waste our substance on negativity and throw away our birthright.

MB: There's the phenomenon of someone like Caravaggio, who has this remarkable power of attention and was totally disorganized in other areas. He had this incredible ability to interpret reality, yet his own life was a willful nightmare. It's very mysterious.

WCS: The mystery we must all take into consideration lies in the moment that transforms everything. What is it in that moment that brings God into our sphere of being? For me, there is this silence. If we're able to evoke this silence, it would be a very clear sign of the presence of a master—not a master in the formal sense, but in our ability to change things around us, to do without doing. It's very difficult to evoke or to sustain, but the great masters are able both to evoke this mysterious opening to the new energy and to sustain it. Gurdjieff used the expression the "Omnipresent Okidanokh."

In the midst of my mechanical living, if I stop and I make contact with my breath, I may be evoking this ever-present okidanokh, which opens us up to a new quality of energy. I've witnessed this in very few people. Gurdjieff could do it. There would be silence in those moments with him where we would possess a much greater attention. This is the mysterious quality that I think the masters possess, either through knowledge, development, or inheritance. The Japanese express this as satori. I recall coming out of a Japanese monastery after two or three months of sitting. I bought a loaf of bread and a box of strawberries on my way to the railway station. As I stood on the platform and took a bite of a strawberry, with the sun hitting my face, I suddenly realized, "Oh, this is what the old boys meant." It was so simple. If we know this secret, we've been able to receive mastership from the masters. If we're prepared not lose it. Otherwise we get distracted. Think of the life we ordinarily lead. No scenery, no real fresh air, no good food.

MB: There are a number of individuals who are recognized as masters because they put their teachings down on paper or lecture about them. The Dalai Lama has both qualities. He has the ability to do what Gurdjieff did, which is to emanate a certain quality. But he also writes and articulates it.

WCS: There are people who are better fitted to opening people up without talk and intellection. And there are others who can express themselves verbally in such a way that a disciple is able to follow and be helped by it.

MB: The real master gives it directly, without articulation.

WCS: The masters are there, if we're ready to recognize them. There are a few. You meet a man and he may seem like a simple man, but he's got something that you would like to know more about. You would like to feel him more. And that's an opening. That raises the question of whether one can be called a master without having a following.

MB: It requires an interaction. Yet they can speak across the ages and have disciples right now. How do we explain that in terms of being a master?

WCS: The call coming from a true master is so strong that it reverberates over the ages, and is able to attract people after the master himself has gone. The teaching is fortified, not by the will of the master, but by the energy with which he imbues everything he says and touches.

MB: Does it have any definite connection with sanctity? Do you have to be a saint before you can become a master or is it irrelevant?

WCS: I can be a great individual, but unless I have that spark or energy which makes contact, nothing essential can develop. I won't really be able to bring about this quality of openness that can help others.

MB: At the end of his life, St. Thomas Aquinas said that all the extraordinary writing he had done was worthless compared with the illumination he had received.

WCS: Yes, all of this wonderful information, as you phrase it, is worth nothing compared to this evocation of a moment, which penetrates to a deeper level.

MB: Instantaneously?

WCS: It has nothing to do with time.

MB: Have you known any other masters?

WCS: I'm trying to visualize my own relationships with different people, and it's difficult to come to someone whom I would irrevocably call a master. I would say, speaking quite honestly, that my relationship with Ouspensky was one of going through a teaching. I imbibed what he had to offer. But for me, he passed along what he knew, but what he knew had been given to him by someone else.

MB: Does one's search continue even if one finds a master? You said earlier that the ultimate master is within yourself. That's where the search ends. But I don't think you ignore help in the process.

WCS: We need help to reach a certain point. But at a later stage, one doesn't believe anything. Neither God nor oneself.

MB: Do you think a master is necessary as a preliminary?

WCS: It's necessary to acquire a certain amount of training, knowledge, and experience, which can be given from one person to another. But there comes a time, as I was saying, when all of the teaching and all that one can give to another doesn't help, so one is left empty, blank. And then he's ready to truly search. He can only find it within himself. I'm sure there are people nowadays who question whether it is worthwhile looking for a master. How do I know if I have found someone who qualifies? What would help me? What kind of contact is necessary with a master? Is there such a thing as a pure spirit that makes one qualified?

MB: We have to be critical. It seems to me there are obviously false masters that are accepted as the true thing.

WCS: Do you know the story of the man who tells his disciples to jump off a cliff? His first disciple jumps over the cliff and lands on his feet unharmed. The second jumps and also lands safely on his feet. The third one jumps and it's the same thing. Now the master leans over the edge of the cliff, thinking these guys should be dead. So he says to himself, gee whiz, I have great power. So he jumps and is killed. I suppose that faith overcomes everything, even a false master.

MB: You met Sai Baba in India. What was your opinion of him?

WCS: My western intellect says he is so obviously a fake it isn't even funny. On the other hand, who am I to judge, when all of a sudden he says, "Give me your hand," and in my hand appears a watch. But my opinion is personal. I can never accept him. But that doesn't mean others can't.

MB: You've also spoken about meeting Muktananda.

WCS: Yes, he straightened out the eyes of my little Siamese cat.

MB: I love that.

WCS: He had a knowledge that I didn't have. For instance, he explained the significance of the fire god in some pieces of sculpture we have. He obviously had a thorough knowledge of these things. But again for me, he was not a master. It's really so subjective. This man believes in a master. Another doesn't. What is it a master gives that doesn't touch you but touches me?

MB: In the past, you've spoken of Jeanne de Salzman, who was connected with the Gurdjieff work. Was there some point in her life where you felt she moved into the category of a master?

WCS: Yes, there was a point where she came into touch with this spark within herself which changed her to the extent where she could look at you and have very different relationship than she had before.

MB: When did this happen?

WCS: She was in her early 60s. She suddenly emerged from being one of us and we began to look up to her. We accepted her. There was no reason for me to accept her in 1947. In fact, I just thought of her as another woman.

A talented woman, certainly when Gurdjieff died she showed acumen, courage, intelligence, and a level of understanding that was impressive to me. Then I was willing to give a little. In the beginning, I had a similar attitude towards Gurdjieff. I wasn't sure at first. To me he was just a man named Smith. But then you have a moment where something passes between you, and you're more inclined to be open, more open to the possibility of his being quite special.

MB: Is there an explanation for that? Can that be artificially produced? Would asceticism be a way of achieving it?

WCS: We could be helped by the study of Milarepa's transformation. How did that come about? At what cost? What eventually made Milarepa a master was the determination to follow, to obey the instructions of his master, Marpa. As you said, Marvin, if a fool persists in his folly, he shall become wise. If I have enough commitment to a course of action, where commitment means a higher level of attention, then I have the possibility of becoming a master.

MB: This rhythm of withdrawing and then feeling at a certain moment that you must go back into the world and make a contribution is what could be called a bodhisattva approach. Are masters bodhisattvas?

WCS: I think a true master doesn't care about anything but persistently relating to this mysterious energy which is always present. He doesn't care whether a formal training exists and whether he has it or not. He's only concerned with his own relationship to the highest. There's a freedom and an openness about him that in turn generates an energy which touches others.

MB: He's generous. He is not reclusive and he doesn't keep it to himself. Otherwise he wouldn't be a master. Do you think generosity is an overflowing of this?

WCS: A master is someone who makes poetry. He doesn't think about it. Like a child artist. He just paints something. He doesn't say "I'm a master." Just as a child doesn't say "I'm going to create." He doesn't even think he's giving anything. As soon as I think I can give you anything, I fall. But if we act just naturally, we come together. And between us arises a feeling that cannot be so easily identified. To have any goals is not it either. It's like that Buddhist sutra: no wisdom, no attainment, no thought, no feeling, no non-feeling, no love, no non-love—until one arrives at that pure emptiness which we are sometimes able to recognize and value. But as soon as we take it seriously and talk about it, we lose it. One must be a master naturally—one does not try to be one. As soon as you try to help, you're lost.

MB: There's no anxiety.

WCS: No anxiety. No ambition. No wish to help. I was taking part in a lecture one time. I made the statement that wishing doesn't help in this work. I was speaking on a rather ordinary level. A woman on the panel responded with a harangue about how it's necessary to have a wish. And I was thinking all the while, this poor woman is being held back by her wish to help others. She was not free of her wish. And I was struck by the fact that any wishing, any desire to become something, any desire to help or change others, is not it.

Roshi Kobori and WCS

MB: No wish, no desire.

WCS: No desire, no wish. Evidently in the life of a human being, there are moments when the purity of the inner world is so great that it needs room for the appearance of something that is truly celestial. What can God be for you and me? As soon as one names it, one has lost it.

MB: It has to do with faith, with confidence in a greater power.

WCS: Isn't faith tinged with mental conception?

MB: You say "Thy will be done." That to me is faith. I trust that whatever's happening has some meaning.

WCS: If you carry out that idea, "thy will be done" it also can signify absolute non-identification.

MB: Freedom.

WCS: Yes. I would say that simple word, "freedom," is closer to it. Freedom unattached to anything, even God. If God appeared now, then I'd punch him in the face. I'd ask Him, what are you doing around here? You're not going to help me, and I'm not going help you. You go your way and I'll go mine. Then I'm open to real freedom. That would be faith.

MB: And then you are open to God. When you reject him, you open yourself.

WCS: All these teachings are full of contradictions. Yet we are given many hints—in the silence. Kobori used to say that between zero and one a soul is born. Now if you ponder that, it's really zero. In other words, what I think he was saying is that between the human being with all his attributes and feelings, and the silence, between me and nothing, a soul is born.

MB: Does it have anything to do with love?

WCS: One has to have the knowledge that enables one to be free of any negative energies. Impatience or anger in me spoils everything. We live in a very delicate, subtle world where every word spoken has its place. I speak and it produces an effect in you. If my words are negative, impatient, or angry, it spoils the relationship. One must have an understanding of one's effect as a human being. Within each of us there is a well of energy that is untapped. One quality of the master is to refine or purify the energy in the people he encounters.

MB: What can we hope for from masters?

WCS: All we can do is prepare ourselves for the encounter. Preparation is very important. Preparing for the advent of a relationship means one has to be more or less pure, a true man. Don't have any dreams of meeting a master. Simply set about preparing yourself.

MB: How can the danger of embracing a false master be avoided? Is there any technique for preventing that?

WCS: We have to be very practical. It requires intelligence. One should have a discriminating mind in order to know the false from the true. But it's difficult. We live in a world where all our values are distorted. We are faced with all sorts of scandals. This is where your discrimination comes in. One hears about some supposed master taking advantage of a young lady. Wouldn't you say that it depends on the individual? On the young woman's own experience? She either grew or she did not. Either she profited by the experience or not.

MB: Are you optimistic about the appearance of masters?

WCS: Yes, I am. If the master doesn't want to deceive people. If he's not acting out of egotism. If he is not trying to gain anything but is trying to live his own life as purely as he can. That way, as an example, he can help others. In that sense, I'm optimistic. On the other hand, if the so-called master is not aware that his every word is having an effect, the results can be quite damaging. But if he acts purely, out of the purity in himself, and the disciple is ready to receive it, I think good can happen.

MB: If you read the *New York Times*, there seem to be very few areas where such a person could emerge. Maybe that in itself is significant.

WCS: I believe there are groups of individuals who are on the right track. I see them come every week and listen to people like me talk. If they do it with an openness week after week, something accrues, and I do notice a transformation. Their being changes. They are able to give a finer quality of attention.

MB: It's important to have a commitment to something of value, something that in itself is a serious endeavor.

WCS: When there are enough people, yes. Certainly in the Gurdjieff work I notice that there are maybe 30 or 40 people who little by little have become more open. I'm optimistic because I see that it takes a long time. And one never knows. I remember one time I expressed impatience with someone in whom I saw so little progress. And a friend said, no, be patient.

MB: Well, there's that story you told about the people jumping over the cliff. You don't know whether this ninny over here is going to suddenly end up way ahead of you.

WCS: That's true, absolutely. We don't know. The master may be behind the counter.

Margaret Segal, 7 years old, with Mr. Gurdjieff in Paris, circa 1947

O. de Hartmann and J. de Salzmann

John Pentland

"She suddenly emerged from being one of us . . ."

J. de Salzmann

IV Going East

Japan

Letters from Japan, 1952

In Paul Reps' book, "Letters to a Friend" written to Bill, the recipient of the letters, tells in a long preface of his first trip to Japan in 1952 with this poet who already knew and loved the Orient, and Japan in particular. The stories are often the same, but in the letters to Cora there is a spontaneity and enthusiasm for this country that became familiar immediately, as if he had known it in a past life (which is what a number of his Japanese friends believed). Japan became essential in Bill's life. He published articles on this trip, and on the numerous ones that followed, and his piles of photographs speak eloquently of Bill's fascination with all aspects of Japanese life, whether it was business or the life of the monasteries. He would tell smilingly of the advice he would give to his Japanese friends, "Don't change a thing in your country. Don't modernize, don't Americanize, it's marvelous as it is." And having tried a Toyota car early on, he told them that Japan would never be a player in the automobile industry and he refused the stocks that were offered to him.

On our first visit to Kyoto, after he had seen his friend Kobori, we took the local train to a suburb, where Bill meditated before his favorite sculpture, the Miroku Bosatsu. He wrote the following description for one of his magazines:

Of all the works of art in Japan, perhaps the most graceful and the most subtle is a wooden statue, living in a small suburb of Kyoto, in the temple of Koryuji. "Miroku," the loveliest statue of a woman, has no breasts, an oversized head and a rather thick neck. Yet so moving is her beauty that people stand transfixed, often moved to tears of joy upon seeing her. It is difficult to understand why this life size wood carving, covered with gilt laquer, has such an effect on those who come to see her. But it is there. It is not her delicate and ineffable grace that impresses, but more a quality which seems to come from a world higher. Her pose is simple. She sits with one leg placed over her thigh. Her right hand is a masterpiece of feminine

On the Hudson River with
D.T. Suzuki

grace. Her arm is thin, her shoulders delicate. But it is her face that enchants and moves... a face that changes as you move slowly around her. Watching her you are transformed. Her ecstatic state conveys itself to you. She is. She exists, more alive than we are.

Today the temple is filled with tourists, and the statue, recognized as a national treasure, has changed place. When Bill saw it for the first time, it was among many other things stuffed in a dusty storeroom, and he was amazed to find a masterpiece there. A picture of Miroku was always near him. When he would be asked what most intrigued him in Zen Buddhism, he would reply, the aesthetics.

One of the strongest impressions in Bill's letters to Cora is his meeting with the redoubtable and powerful president of Kanebo, Itoji Muto. This important man apparently developed a spontaneous confidence and friendship for the young American who was so open to Japanese civilization and its people. As with Ouspensky, D. T. Suzuki, Orozco and many of the special people he met, Bill had this capacity to forge close ties immediately.

This presence which Bill emanated was obvious not only in the business world but also in the spiritual domain. The priests and abbots of all the monasteries which Bill visited, thanks to introductions from D. T. Suzuki, all became true friends. They never passed through New York without visiting him, and the doors of their monasteries were open to him at all times.

In Chester

I lead a double life

After the war, Dr. Daisetz Suzuki had begun his lectures on Japan at Columbia University and I thought it might be good to have an article in *Gentry*, which was running philosophical articles. The first article about "Hands" appeared in *Gentry* (see appendix). I went to Dr. Suzuki's office with Christopher Fremantle. Dr. Suzuki knew Anne Fremantle. Fremantle asked the first few questions. But I could see that I was on a beam with Suzuki right from the start. We continued to have a strong relationship. He knew I was interested in Gurdjieff and Ouspensky. I invited him to see the Movements at Franklin Farms, where he spoke to the group — and in private to Madame Ouspensky.

Dr. Suzuki liked to get around. I took him on a trip on the Hudson Line, and he came to Chester where he spent a number of weekends. The day arrived that I was to go to Japan, and he responded enthusiastically that he would help me with introductions to a number of Zen masters. He wrote six letters of introduction to three Rinzai monasteries and to three Soto Zen temples. Here I must bring Paul Reps into the picture. Paul Reps had been writing stories for *American Fabrics* and *Gentry* and in one of his notes to me, accompanying an article, he mentioned he was going again to Japan. Could we go together? As his dates corresponded to the trip I was planning, we decided to spend a few weeks together in Japan. The trip from New York to Tokyo took three days with stop-offs in Los Angeles, Hawaii and Wake Island. I recall very vividly my first impression of the land of Japan as the big B-24 bomber came in over the bay of Tokyo. It was a spring morning and the sun shone on the green land with extraordinary intensity. I entered Japan with a feeling for its beauties and possibilities.

(from letters to Cora Segal)
Beautiful individual rooms are given to us and we are certainly being thrown into the real Japan. (Paul and I are the only ones who can speak English.)

We are immediately taken to the home of one of Japan's foremost musicians—at the moment I forget his name. Fabulous character but cannot speak English. He has 12 disciples living in his house, studying music. One plays for us during tea. Then his daughter entertains—wonderful player on the "Koto," a sort of a sit-down bull fiddle. The house is elegant with old Japanese gardens, etc.

At 5 o'clock, Paul, I and the musician, with an interpreter and another friend, sit down for a meal. The wife stays in the background, beautiful in her dignity and old Japanese robes. We sit around a square table which covers a hole in the floor where you can drop your legs in case you get tired from cross-legged position.

Second day in Japan. Had good night's sleep. Practiced Japanese Zen meditation. Breakfasted on strawberries. So far, no American in sight. Two medicine men (and you should see us!) have a very heavy program. Luckily I began to have a few words in Japanese I am able to use. Gentleness and politeness are all around and the people everywhere seem unusually sweet. How they even could have fought a war is hard to understand. Incidentally, their material resources seem so poor you wonder why we didn't beat them in a month. None of America's great material strength is in evidence and if China and Russia are being blown up as to their strength, I would not be surprised.

Just a line or two to tell you a little about this Never-Never Land. It is unbelievable unless you are here.

For example, this morning after spending the night in one Shinto temple, I had breakfast with the head priest, and took a bath that mother would have loved —so hot and in a tub twice as deep as ours. I wear very luxurious under and over kimonos. Very chic. So then the priest gets out a camera and one of the young priests takes our photo in front of various old shrines. Of course this is a small town temple.

Thomi De Hartmann — ...leave let me... musical recital there

NO1. Court Music

Older man and young
kneel before beautiful gold
screen and play.
Plaintive notes.
Young mans accomp-
animent is much
Softer, more feminine

gold screen as
back point

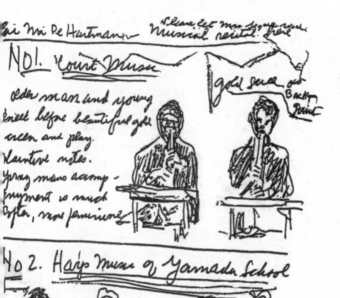

No 2. Harp Music of Yamada School

(4) flute
is
alone

Two Koto
& guitar
& flute } 4 people

Koto
#1

(Koto #2)

(SA-MISEN)
guitar

Low singing very, very soft Sad - long single
notes on Koto. Like a continuous wail with
punctuation of the strings instrument
The Two Koto players play together - Same chords
Sometimes Koto Female Singer - Then Guitar Female Player

Indian
fashion
audience

Played by blind musicians in
very FRAGILE STYLE.

VIOLIN PLAYER
STANDS — KOTO PLAYER
SITS

KOTO PLAYER OFTEN PLAYS NOTES OR
SMALL MELODIES WHICH ARE DUPLICATED BY
THE VIOLIN PLAYER. OFTEN THEY SEEM TO
TALK TO ONE ANOTHER - VIOLIN TO KOTO. THIS ONE
SEEMED MORE MODERN. AUDIENCE LIKED VERY MUCH

No. 4. NA GAUTA

FLUTE AND PIANO
FLUTE PLAYS HIGH
NOTES PIANO LOW

THESE 2 PERFORMERS
ARE VERY
YOUNG

ALL THE MUSIC SEEMS SAD WITH SMALL
INTERJECTIONS OF LIGHT PASSAGES. BUT EVERY
ONCE IN A WHILE VERY GAY CHEERFUL PASSAGES
THAT ARE MELODIUS HELP TO GIVE CONTEMPORARY
COLOR TO WHAT MUST HAVE ORIGINALLY BEEN
VERY OLD FORMALIZED STYLE.

T. de Hartmann

Now he takes me to a village festival where ten young girls in beautiful costumes have arranged special flower arrangements. They were truly fine. Then after going through a long lane like a village bazaar, it ends up at the temple of the Zen sect where the monks are waiting to show me around. It is a beautiful austere temple almost a perfect architectural gem. The monks show me around, we have tea, inspect lovely gardens etc. Always much bowing and you have to learn to sit on floor. The floors are simple matting about two inches thick. Breakfast is fascinating with its shrimp dishes—and always tea, rice and seaweed. Every place you go shoes must be off as the floors are beautiful polished wood or straw matting. All is simple, dignified and exquisite.

And the children! You will understand why they make so many Japanese dolls if you see the children. Each one is a doll.

I wrote that Japan is a Never-Never-Land. By some queer chance I found myself climbing to the top of a high mountain near Miyashima. A very interesting Japanese by the name of Tokuzan (he was recommended by Suzuki and was formerly head of National Diet's library) was accompanying us. After a hard three-hour climb (luckily I am in good shape and had good shoes) we reach the top. Another monastery of some obscure Buddhists—beautiful with wonderful carvings. How they ever got materials to build, I will never know.

They agreed to put us up for the night and who do you think is the head of this temple? A seeress—an old woman with 300 followers. She goes into trances, waves her hands and gives guidance to those people who follow her. Very old, spare—she is known as grandmother of the mountains. Some girl!

Tokuzan speaks with her and I delighted her by drawing her picture and giving it to her with a flourish. We arranged to sleep in the temple. They always have bedding and floor space. Loveliest bedroom I've ever seen . . . looking over what is the finest view in the world. I have small sketches which I will bring home.

She gets fonder of me as I talk through Tokuzan and then after a hot bath in a very primitive rock bath filled with hottest water I've ever had and a young boy priest washing my back—Supper.

Hot sake which the seeress pours out herself very frequently. A truly magnificent meal . . . fresh bamboo shoots, rice, peas, cucumber, delicious bean sprout soup, egg mixture, wild potatoes, etc. all with sake and then three kinds of tea—ending with ginger root (not crystallized). Meanwhile, she doesn't eat but pours sake and smokes out of a tiny pipe. (I hope it wasn't opium.) Then her followers eat—after she chants a prayer and they all repeat after her and clap hands several times. It is a wonderful atmosphere and we are all gay as larks.

So here I am at the top of the mountain and we are now waiting for them to finish. The seeress says that she will wake up at two in the morning and go to the shrine to make a secret practice of her religion. I asked if I could see but she says 'no'—no one sees— Because at 3:30 a.m. she gets her communication from the Divinity. She is so serious about it and is such a sweet old woman, I am inclined to believe her. Her 300 followers believe in her implicitly.

WCS and Paul Reps

P.S. I cannot stop without telling you—She told me —spirits are alive in the world. She is in communication with them. Quite fantastic. But she is a sincere old woman.

Further notes on the seeress:

Last night she had an idiot boy about ten years old whom she said was deaf and dumb hovering about us.

About 6 o'clock in the morning, I was awakened by a wild chanting. I got up and climbed up to the place where there is a small Buddha alter. The so-called dumb boy was circling around the altar repeating some prayer and making a bow before the Buddha each time.

It was really weird as he did not know I was watching. It was rather impressive too in that wild mountain setting.

Well, from breakfast on I kept after the seeress and here is the afterthought on what I wrote about last night.

On our way up we were screened first at a large Buddhist monastery. Remember this was after we came recommended by Tokuzawan's brother with whom we spent the night and who is the head abbot of his own monastery. We go up the mountain to a small hut to ask if we get a place to sleep at the top. The small hut is staffed with three old ladies who we later found out are part of the lady priest's group. Then the old lady herself, acting like anybody, serves us a wonderful meal . . . As I wrote, she became very friendly (of course we are at top of the world in grand scenery—nature at its greatest) and she probably never saw a white man before. But let me go on and give you the dope as it is interesting.

There were three middle-aged women in the room —all very intelligent, alert & alive and very serene. But she was the boss. One of them is to be the head priestess after she dies. They reminded one of Ms. Pearson and Miss Harper. The other one was a weekly visitor from the mainland below and just as we, she had a large business and servants of her own at home but she climbs up the mountain to work with the seeress. The other people do likewise but the first two are always with the priestess. When men come up to visit her, they do—guess what—mostly cut wood and repair the small temple. People are helped in their troubles, I was told, when they came.

The priestess herself showed me the cave where she spent three years alone & meditating. It was unbelievable. You and I could not spend an hour there. It looks out over an awesome view and she said she too was frightened when thunder and lightening would hit against the rocks. She is a tiny woman, too.

She also did a small service for us before the Buddha altar—very beautiful to watch and very sincere and moving. She blessed me in a good way and said I would be fortunate. Said she had her ideas in her heart but cannot tell them in words and that she is very happy and serene in her religious work.

Further note. She calls two crows to her on a flute. They are trained to come up from sea level at her call.

Still further. After we left, I met her on the streets of a town looking like any Japanese woman going shopping. She often goes into life that way. But I will have more to tell so be patient.

After a 15 hour railroad ride we arrived to spend the night at the place I am writing from—a Sien Temple, Branch of Shinto Buddhism—not Zen. The abbot was thrilled to have us—very special persons Reps and I—having come from America. We sleep in a fantastically lovely pavilion in an austere room and the atmosphere is really special, if only because of its serenity and cut-offness from the world. It is a very old temple but small and they get few people from out-side.

The abbot and the two of us had breakfast in real-ly grand style—wonderful food served by the two priests in spectacular robes. The whole set-up is love-ly except I don't think—but of course I am not sure—that they know the answers. A good deal of chanting, gong banging and meditating but while it has a quiet serene atmosphere it is not alive in the way we know it and the way it must have been hundreds of years ago. But I have not yet reached Suzuki's temples so I am hopeful. I have my letters of introduction trans-lated and he really went all out to give me his highest recommendation in his introductions.

The little village here is quite charming. I was pre-sented previously today to the Mayor of the town who made a study of Nestorians in China. He is going to

Cora dear:
Pine tree
outside my
room is
exquisite...
Everything
here. detto.
Please leave
Paisley Type
enclosed +
hold for gentry
Tell Liz I have
bought her small
jade
hope
Bill

"My room at Fu-ku-da-ya in Tokyo was sparse in furniture but had its own private garden."

give me a paper in English which he wrote on this subject as he is considered the greatest living scholar on Nestorians who I have a vague idea were early Christians. Ask de Hartman about them. The Mayor is 85 years old, by the way. Also went to a Japanese kindergarten—the kids are wonderful to watch.

Reps was relatively unknown in the U.S., but deeply appreciated in Japan. Receptions and dinners inundated us for several weeks. But I intended to take time to visit Dr. Suzuki's Zen Monasteries. As Paul did not agree with the rigidity of this formal Buddhism, we decided to go our separate ways. "Don't go, they'll spoil you," he used to say.

I returned to Tokyo for a summing up of my voyage and to gather myself as to my future course. As publisher of *American Fabrics*, I had had a natural contact with the silk and textile industry in Japan. The American government was particularly anxious to encourage the silk export business of Japan. Various programs had been discussed in New York to foster this trade between the two nations, so I had some openings, through the magazine, with Japanese textile companies. One morning, while I was at my hotel in Tokyo, I received a telephone call from Mr. Kimura. He was the secretary of Mr. Itoji Muto, the president of Kanebo, the great Japanese textile firm located in Osaka. Over the telephone he asked me if we could meet and he mentioned that Mr. Muto of Kanebo would be happy to discuss some matters with me.

Mr. Kimura and I got on famously from the beginning. At that time, as one will recall, not too many Americans spoke Japanese. Kimura was a Harvard graduate and a very cultured man, and certainly had had a great experience with America and its people and customs. We became friendly and after a meeting or two he asked me: "Mr. Segal, why do you stay in a hotel which is the equivalent of a New York City hotel?" What was he after? It came out that Mr. Muto, whom I had not yet met, was indirectly advising that I stay at a Japanese inn to be acquainted with a Japanese atmosphere. I had been in many small Japanese inns but had not thought of going outside of a modern hotel in Tokyo. Mr. Kimura suggested that I take up residence at the Fukudaya. With his help, arrangements were made.

A car was put at my disposal, and took me and my few belongings to the Ryokan. I was amazed by the elegance and at the same time simplicity and aesthetic beauty of this Japanese inn. I go further: I fell in love with it. It gave me a sense of tranquility and isolation, and a relationship with the Japanese which I could never have had in the Tokyo business hotel.

I had spent a few days there writing notes, collecting myself, when I received another message from Mr. Kimura: Mr. Muto would be pleased to have me come to Osaka for a business talk. Mr. Kimura added that perhaps we could even take the trip from Tokyo to Osaka together. This was an agreeable proposal: how often could I have a chance to meet a Japanese on such close terms, and with one who spoke English as well as Mr. Kimura did?

We flew to Osaka. Astonishment was my first reaction to the airport. After the end of the war, Osaka airport itself consisted of a small two-story building with a couple of rooms and very primitive airport facilities. But when we arrived, there was a rather impressive black limousine—in it, two important looking personages, both part of the Kanebo secretariat to the President. I recall vividly the ride into the city. Just outside the airport was a settlement of nightclubs and bars for the American enlisted men who were stationed nearby. Usually these types of establishment are what they are, dreary looking. I do recall that these were, in their own way, charming. They did not have the sordid quality and drabness that I was accustomed to seeing in other parts of the world where similar situations catering to men away from home prevailed. We entered an area of rice paddies and farm houses; a picture of great beauty, for a short while. Fairly soon we entered another industrial zone where, for the first time, I saw a smoke stack

Second in command at Eiheiji

region. I was struck by the simplicity and crudity of these smokestacks and of the industrial buildings, all more of less powered by coal and wood, all more or less gray, grim looking. It was a far cry from the beauty of the landscapes which I had encountered by the airport. We drove into the city. Mr. Kimura had me settled in the "Kanomori," the Emperor's brother's favorite ryokan. In this quiet and artistic environment I was immediately at ease and felt at home like at the "Fukudaya" in Tokyo.

Everything here that shows beauty is of the highest order. When I get home, I will probably take up the profession of landscape gardener or architect. We are babes in the wood compared to the Japanese but you have to see it to really appreciate their beautiful sense of living.

My own quarters are fascinating. Three maids are assigned to me. When I come home they strip my clothes off, adjust my kimonos, serve hot facial towels, tea, press my pants, etc. laundry and what have you. It is embarrassing, they are so sweet and kind.

The meals here would interest you. They serve dishes that look like floral arrangements on a small exquisite scale. The people, are very gentle and innocent in many ways. You begin to see how hard, tough and ungentle we Americans are. A brusque movement here could break up a good part of a house which is composed of lovely fragile woods and paper. Their food is infinitely better than ours—no vital foods in America, compared to the fish (infinite varieties) right out of the sea, lakes, rivers which are everywhere. Also you would enjoy their bathrooms: that's where they really go to town. The most important room is their bathroom with wide large deep tubs for really hot baths and many other interesting and architectural effects. Their toilets, where you have to squat, are very integrally designed and are always immaculate. Even fine small flower arrangements in these toilets.

Eiheiji

A strong faith is needed to begin work. A very determined mind is needed to continue.

97

The next day, Mr. Kimura suggested a meeting with Mr. Muto. It was a memorable trip from the Ryokan to the Kanebo headquarters in Yodogawa. As we drove into the precincts of the company, I was again overwhelmed by the beauty of the grounds themselves. The planting of the trees, the flowerbeds, the whole atmosphere was very impressive to an American who was accustomed to rather conventional business offices, certainly not located in the middle of a spacious park.

I sensed a special atmosphere coming from the attitudes of the employees, who were all very neatly attired (prevalence of white gloves throughout the Kanebo offices). This carried at each step, from the greetings of the young girls, with their immaculate uniform, to the elevator operator, to the secretarial staff. I was ushered into the office of the president, on the top floor of a five-story building. On first coming into these quarters, I could immediately feel the elegant taste of the office, and looked forward to the meeting with anticipation. This was my first introduction to Kanebo's Yodogawa plant and to Mr. Muto. Mr. Muto is an extremely impressive looking, powerful man with a leonine head. At the same time one sensed a kindliness about him. He spoke English very well, as he had been educated in England. I felt a sympathetic character in him. He mentioned my Buddhist experiences—at that time rather brief—with the Zen people. He was acquainted with Dr. Suzuki who lived in Kita Kamakura, where Mr. Muto's own family had a home. We spoke about cultural and aesthetic matters and it was a very pleasant interview. He still did not explain why he wanted to see me, but I could assume that I was fairly well known because of *American Fabrics*. I did venture to ask him why he should wish to see me, and he said that a mutual friend in America named Abbot Copeland, who was the head of United Merchants and Manufacturers Organization, had suggested that the two of us would get along well together, perhaps because of our mutual interest in textiles and in art. I was sure when we parted that we would meet again. Then, on to my ryokan where I spent a few more days, and I embarked again on visiting Zen monasteries, which was the primary purpose of my trip to Japan.

One of the places I was very anxious to visit (and possibly stay a few weeks) was Eiheiji, head of the Soto sect. This monastery, located in the Echizen province, was founded by Dogen Zenji in 1243. It was not easy for a foreigner to move around the country in the postwar period. It was summer, the weather was warm, I traveled in an old chino suit. I would frequently contact the nearest American military post where I could get a jeep or a small car. A driver would be at my disposal to take me to the temples I wished to visit. The arrival to Eiheiji was memorable.

(from letters to the magazine)
Eiheiji is far off from Tokyo in a little village in the mountains. How I got here without guide or interpreter is a story in itself.

I arrived in the village in a small electric car at night. I showed my letter to the station master and immediately things began to happen. The conductor walked up the hill with me and I was introduced at the monastery office. Then a series of monks, much conversation and finally I am let in, evidently as some through an interminable number of buildings and up and up, steps on steps. It was climbing up a mountain. Finally we got to the top of one large building and were greeted by a distinguished looking monk in a different color robe than the black which the Zen monks wore.

We sat in a room for about ten minutes. Then another monk signaled us into a beautiful room with walls covered in blue silk. Then the head Abbot comes in smiling benevolently, and we had tea—it was about 8 at night. Two more big shots—you can tell them by robes—and faces—came in and it was very good. We were all relaxed and quiet and the atmosphere was alive without being heavy. They asked me how long I wished to stay, but conversation was almost impossible because of the language difficulty.

After about half an hour they said my room was ready, and the heads and two assistants took me to another lovely room, large and austere, but very charming details of flowers and pictures.

A monk who can speak Esperanto is my only contact, but somehow we are getting along. They seem to be very happy to have an outsider come in—especially one sent by Dr. Suzuki. We sat around for a couple of hours the first night. The kitchen sent up a meal for me—they knew I had been travelling all day. By 11 p.m. the young monk had made up my bed and prepared my robe, etc., and at 12 I was asleep. At 3:30 a.m. I was up saying morning prayers with a large group. They have a very rigorous schedule—but they all seem very healthy—and they are relaxed, quiet and serene. The atmosphere is very masculine, which is very nice. I fit in without trouble—they all seem to be "regular" as the saying goes.

It is like living in a college for advanced students except that many of the monks are older men. The simple life evidently keeps them healthy (the ones who told me they were 60 and 65 looked about 45). The toilet and washrooms are all immaculate as are the kitchens. The grounds are absolutely out of the world and my room always has fresh flowers. I will give you the set-up in later letters, as I cannot easily get someone to post my mail. They do not get out of the grounds too often, so I have to wait for an opportunity.

There are about a hundred monks, I judge, but I may be wrong. I am living in the top echelon corridor—three colonels and myself have large wonderful rooms across a courtyard from the rest of the monks. Where the Master and his assistants sleep, I do not know. I have tried to keep alert and learn what I can, but I really need the language.

I just had a big surprise. A special delegation to escort me to a new big room which is to be my "laboratory." I think the report went out that I am engaged in important work and need an extra study —with the only table in the place. Very fancy with rich covered walls—but I will probably continue to work in the first room. Evidently writing is regarded highly.

After being here for several days, I confess I am stumped. Unquestionably they are riding on a great teaching and tradition. All the evidence, atmosphere, etc. indicate that the Zen Masters really knew or know something. I have been able to see a great deal, having complete freedom. You know how I like to be behind the scenes. The most impressive place is the Zazen Hall. It has 96 mats where the monks do their meditation, living, sleeping, etc. Now I have the feeling they only use it for meditation. I described the 3:30 in the morning performance. It gives evidence of real work having gone on in its precincts. The monks themselves do many of the things such as sensing, trying to be aware. They are also quick and give great service. They are very friendly and they congregate in my room—very free in showing me pictures, trying to tell me what a limited language exchange permits. They love photographs and want to know all about my family, etc. They are continually bringing me small gifts which are warmly given. The top echelon consisting of the Master, the 2nd in command and the third one are way above the average. The Master gave me a beautiful gift of a hand-bound book and several smaller things on the second day. The third in command was born the son of a priest and has been one all his life—very intelligent and quick. Many of the young men are also sons of monks of other temples who came here because it is supposed to be the best Zen monastery. Physically the place is large, spacious and lovely. You see the results of hundred(s) of years of effort and care.

The monks have their pots of charcoal fire with tea kettles going all the time. Delightful place socially to drop in and talk, read, rest, etc. Despite rigorous schedule I am feeling wonderful.

My brother monk who is assigned to me is sup-

posed to wake me at 3:30 a.m. He is a nice fellow but his superiors don't trust his translation as he can only understand and speak Esperanto. I communicate directly with gestures, etc. It's a ritual every morning—rush to the toilet and wash up and then to the 3:45 meditation. This is a lulu! and quite impressive. About 40 monks seated like Westpointers in Pasmasanah positions facing the wall. About 10 minutes of silence, then an older, obviously intelligent teacher talks for about 10 minutes. Prior to the beginning I am instructed on the technique of sitting. They are lenient with me. They sit ramrod stiff: hands folded thumb nails touching, nose lined up with center of body, ears in line with shoulders. One monk walks with a stick, very formal, stiff. If a head dozes or even goes out of position—crack over the right shoulder with the stick. This too is a ritual which they showed me and even let me practice. After the lecture they merely sit while a gong is periodically struck to bring their attention back to themselves. Near the end, a drum is beaten—very effective. We sit 40-45 minutes without moving. Morning and evening. I am able to do it quite easily except my mind does wander. But the gong's vibrations help bring you back. It was an important holiday today so we have about 200 visitors from other temples, and several services were preformed. These services are very impressive since the monks are well drilled, and they use these public occasions to further work on themselves as we do at movement demonstrations. They have work to do in between morning and evening meditation but they also have plenty of time to relax in their rooms. I visit freely with them and we talk, smoke and drink tea, all in a friendly non-religious atmosphere. There is also a large private meditation hall where the brothers practice if they wish. As I said, the place is magnificently situated among tall pines in the mountains. It was the favorite of many of the emperors, so it is very rich materially.

About the stick at meditation—it is also used to check on your position and the job of checking is very

serious. After each blow the monk wielding the stick makes a prayer gesture.

I have ducked my brother guide and get along by myself but he will find me soon.

I get daily work memos from the Esperanto brother—something like: "Tymoro morning get up 5:45 komence the ceremonio."

One day I went to a nearby village to buy things to eat. For 3 cents I got the equivalent of 3 boxes of the most delicious strawberries, 6 fresh cucumbers for

1/2 cent and one bread for 1/2 cent. Of course this is in yen—but you can get an idea of how cheap it would be to live here if you were a Japanese villager with a little American money. In the cities and when you are a foreigner it is quite different. When I take a streetcar, incidentally, the fare is also about 1/2 cent.

Some special ceremony took place today as there were a lot of visiting dignitaries—abbots from other temples. The Master sent word that he would not have tea with me but instead sent a beautiful book as a gift. The boys now gather in my room as it is so much more comfortable than theirs on this rainy day. They show me Zen postures and I tell them about USA. I don't know how bright they are as the language gets in the way but they sure can meditate—they sit for an hour without batting an eye. I am very well fed as they keep the trays coming in and the head of the kitchen likes to chew the fat—with his four English words.

Zen monastery politics: I wish to take a hot bath (the bath here is like our Finnish Bath in grandeur). So I go to the one that the brothers use—very fine, too. But as I am about to get in I am stopped—I have to use the special one that is used by the Master and the top Brass. The only trouble is the Head Man and his chief assistant like to use it first. So I have to wait until they are finished—meanwhile the other bath is not being used. Tomorrow is a special holiday so we sleep till 5:00 o'clock. No meditation at 3:30 as usual. The boys put in a tough day from 3:30 a.m. to 9:00 p.m. which is bedtime but they all look well. A 65 year old monk beats me up long flights of stairs. They have wonderful food (outside of rice, I don't know what I'm eating) but no fish or meat—many strange vegetables which they claim they pick in the forest which surrounds the temples. I also get a small pitcher of hot sake—and I give half of it to the two brothers who wait on me. No meat, but sake is OK. Every one of them does a perfect lotus position. They receive a lot of help from women pilgrims who come mornings to clean, sew, etc. It is on a big scale.

Beside outside maintenance of the buildings and a little landscape gardening the monks do not have much heavy work. They do act as lecturers, guides, etc. for the visitors and there are a number of temples that are always in use—need someone to hit the gongs, beat the drums and burn the incense. The ceremonies seem superficial—much like the Judeo-Christian, Greek Orthodox as far as litanies, etc. I have an idea that Zen does not take this part too seriously but does it to keep up appearances and win people's support. What with kitchen, cleaning (everything is wonderfully clean—except in some of the private rooms) there is enough for an 18 hour day. They do seem healthy enough, I saw one very impressive little ceremony that was just like a Noh play - TALKING WITH INTENTION.

They are always emphasizing that one's daily life holds out possibilities and that even in one day one can attain the seed of Buddhahood.

Despite all the strangeness it is still interesting how there is a Japanese counterpart for every American—same levels of being, etc.; same types, same destinies it seems. Evidently God creates the people of the world to fall within strict categories in their essential aspect despite great differences of race, customs, surrounding , etc.

I had a wonderful visit there and it was after several weeks at Eiheiji that I came closer to what might be called a better understanding of what the meaning of Buddhism is.

An amusing occurrence took place at the end of my visit. I had become popular, and even engaged in activities such as woodcutting with the younger men. On the first occasion I went into the woods with them, they were evidently under orders not to subject me to too hard work, not to jeopardize me through accident, and were joking about how well they could chop wood. It just so happens that I am an excellent woodsman myself. But as a lark I suggested that they let me try and see if I could do a little woodchopping. I took one of the axes and gave them a virtuoso display of expert woodchopping and they were amazed. They asked me how come a Zen-American-scholar and writer could do so well with woodchopping. I jokingly replied that all American boys are brought up with axes and saws, therefore we are all specialists from the very beginning. I think they really believed that every American is an expert woodsman before I was through with them.

When it was time for me to leave, the monks gave a party in my room and announced that several of them, including the second-in-command would accompany me to the railroad station to see me off. Before I boarded the train they offered me a large package. Once alone, I discovered that it was two bottles of whisky. Where they found American whisky at that time is a mystery to me, but evidently they thought it was the best present to give me (even though I was not the "ordinary"-type American).

Well Mr. Muto finally caught up with me and for the last two days I lead a double life. I get up at about 5:30 a.m. to take a train to Kamakura, where I have made a good friend of the Chief Abbot, Roshi Asahina and some of the young monks. The Chief Abbot is one of the few real men I have met. Tremendous power yet a regular fellow in many ways—very satisfactory to talk with him. Then back to Tokyo in time for lunch at the Imperial Hotel with the big businessmen and to ride around in a chauffeured Cadillac with Mr. Muto or with his secretary who has nothing to do but see that I am taken care of. It is really embarrassing. Mr. Muto wishes to make my program and was really mad, according to one of his secretaries, that I did not show up when he expected me. To make matters worse, he said he had been hearing about me from Kyoto to Tokyo (which is almost all of Japan)—but no Segal showing at Kanebo. Everyone is flabbergasted that I traveled to remote interior places alone—and that I have been living at Japanese inns instead of foreign hotels.

The boys at one Zen place claimed I have the look of the Boddidharma and had some fun posing me in front of one of their drawings (very sacriligious). I needed a shave—so did Dharma.

One day I was visiting Mr. Muto in his office, we were having some coffee and Mr. Kimura asked: "Mr. Segal, Mr. Muto would like very much for you to consider working as a consultant for our company. Would you be interested?" At that time I was fully engaged and had never anticipated doing work for anybody else but my own company. However, I was so truly intrigued and charmed by the attitude and having resolved that I would spend two or three weeks, I then gave my full attention to what I was doing and forgot for the time about Zen, art, and travel.

It was a very exciting period. I could see and feel the enthusiasm of the Kanebo staff, no matter what the area of business, whether it was the man who swept the office or the head of department, they were always giving their utmost. There was no "shirking", no diversion from the task at hand. The devotion of the people to the company impressed me. One could feel, too, the wave of the future for this company because they were forward minded, willing to take suggestions, willing to experiment and actualize ideas which were put forth.

At the station.

Then we went to Mr. Muto's private museum of the most fabulous ancient fabrics—thousands of rare pieces —in a specially built steel and concrete structure.

Dinner was splendiferous with four Geisha girls. Two were sensationally beautiful (if you did not look beyond their wonderful make-up and lovely costumes) and two were "merely charming." There were five other men besides myself and about eight maids to serve us. The Geisha girls are traditional charmers and entertainers and at the dinner there is no surreptitious sex or flirting. They are there to help the men enjoy themselves so that at the end of the evening they (the men) are relaxed, friendly and can talk business. At least that's the way I saw it. The girls sing and dance and do innocent little tricks like making paper dolls, slight of hand, etc., and the men are quite respectful and friendly in a detached sort of way. They dance very well and at the end of the evening sat

Asahina was the head roshi of the Engakuji and probably the leading figure of Zen Buddhist Rinzai Sect. He was the roshi who sent me a letter addressed to the Pope and insisted that I delivered the letter which he said will help the peace of the world. Asahina's teaching was very rigorous.

—WCS

A Happy New Year to you!
1957 The Cock Year

All my smiling brethren gathered here from all quarters;

We all greet the newly risen sun at the Illumination Hall (Komyo-den, Meditation Hall in Engaku-ji).

I offer a stick of incense to the Buddha,

Praying for the welfare of all mankind:

May the gentle spring breeze blow therefrom

All over the four oceans.

　　　　　　　　　—Asahina Sogen
　　　　　　　　　　to Mr. and Mrs. Segal

around quietly while we talked the strategy of selling textiles throughout the world.

Back to Zen for a moment—I have the strangest feeling that it will have to receive its stimulus in the future from America. It is too hard and too intellectual for the average Japanese—and almost impossible to attempt without spending time making an extraordinary effort in a Zen monastery. They have about 15 million Zen Buddhists mainly among the upper classes—or rather most of the upper classes—former nobility, samurai, etc., are Zen first in religion. But to go through Zen training is too much for most of them. Zen lacks, in my opinion, Gurdjieff's recognition that we live in a modern world—whether we like it or not—the realization of oneself must be made possible in life. Zen believes, too, in work in life, but does seem to demand the intensive training period. I think they may find a hard core of Americans and Europeans who may be willing to go the whole hog, and the Westerners may bring the Japanese into the Zen picture the way they evidently were centuries ago. Their periods of self-remembering or Zazen in depth and time are worth investigating for ourselves, as this is personal experience—the only experience that really matters. We really do talk too much, consider too much, identify too much, all because we have not had the experience that only deep and prolonged sitting (and I don't mean ten minutes twice a day) can bring to one.

I carried Dr. Suzuki's letter to the top of a tremendous range of mountains where there are 60 important Buddhist temples. Mrs. Suzuki spent ten years here—so Suzuki is very well known. The place is about three hours from Osaka.

We were met after a cable car which took you to the top after the regular train. Shojo-in monastery was the first stop. The abbot was a fine man who looked younger than I but who later I learned was 70 years old. The mountain air is so pure and the surroundings

Kanebo archery team

so lovely, I can see how you keep your fresh complexion here. We were almost immediately escorted up a labyrinth to his room (always in the right part of the house). It made a wonderful picture as he wore a violet robe with a white underrobe against the wild mountain background. The whole color scheme, exterior and interior was exquisite and I had an impulse to paint it.

We talked for over an hour about the difference between Shingon and Zen Buddhism. The center of gravity is in "I" or "Self" with Shingon stressing that "Self" is and is in all and all is in Self. In other words Self is and has an interrelationship with all other things and beings both in time and space. The whole lives in and through the individual and the individual permeates the whole. Egoism and identifications result from ignorance of this truth. The contradictions and the oppositions in the world we know are a necessary condition for all existence. At the same time the development of Self or rather recognition in the real sense of Who I AM is possible only because of the existence of this sameness. I hope you get the idea—it seemed very clear when the old man spoke. They—the Shingon sect (which, by the way, translates—True Words—the Esoteric Buddhism) have their own methods, which again are largely concerned with attention and awareness—that stress concentration through a combination of meditation plus prayer.

After an hour or so of talk it was announced that the abbot, Kimura and I would go to another monastery near by. This one was really out of this world for grandeur and beauty. It was built by Hideyoshi, the great Japanese Emperor-maker.

Well, there is so much to write about their attitudes, about their relationship with Zen. These monks think Zen is too severe or, rather, unnecessarily hard-edged in concept and approach, but they feel the two are in the same line. They are very simple and they stress humility more than Zen.

Cora:
all the monks live
in the most beautiful
surroundings. Poor
food but tremendous
vibrations because of
atmosphere. Love Biiep

Margaret, Cora, Mr. Kimura

Japan – the 1960s

On his second trip to Japan, Bill was accompanied by his wife and his eldest daughter, Margaret, then fifteen years old. It was one party after another. And the presents, the loveliest kimonos, precious silks, rare laquerware created especially for the Americans, bamboo baskets and other artistic objects, all were offered with enormous elegance. It was the beginning of a collaboration and friendship which was to endure for a half century.

With the kind of luck that seemed to accompany him all his life, the financial losses created by Gentry *were offset by the fact that "Segal-San" had become an indispensable counselor to Kanebo. During his many business trips to Japan, Bill maintained his contacts with Japanese Zen Buddhism, which exercised an every-growing fascination.*

During this period both Kanebo and Japan were going through rapid changes, documented by Bill as articles in American Fabrics *and* Gentry. *The marriage of Kanebo-Dior, arranged by Bill was a first international license.*

Bill's original mind is made vivid in letters devoted to many different subjects. Here we quote some sections of these long letters meant often for the magazines. Bill developed a great taste for Chinese and Japanese art through his friendship with Mr. Muto (whose collection was famous).

Bill continued to visit D.T. Suzuki who had returned to Japan and now lived in Kita Kamakura - Mihoko Okamura, who is often mentioned, wrote (in the late 1990's) several books on the time she spent with D.T. Suzuki, since she met him at Columbia University when she was fifteen years old and stayed with him until he died in 1969.

While he worked in Osaka, Bill often took the commuter train to Kyoto, in the evening, to attend meditations led by Mrs. Ruth Sasaki, an American who had married a famous Roshi and who had become the first lady Zen priest heading a temple at the Daitoku-ji monastery. Both her meditations and her dinners, which were famous, are the subjects of several letters in this chapter.

Through Paul Reps, Bill met a great Zen priest, Soen Nakagawa. It is to his monastery, Ryutaku-ji, that Bill took Madame de Salzmann to persuade her of the great value of Zen practice of meditation.

Mr. Kimura and WCS waving goodbye to Margaret and Cora

It was one party after another...

Garden parties, Noh parties, geisha parties . . . kimono gift and ceramic making parties, showing the crafts of Japan, were particularly interesting. Overnight firing and glazing of ceramics. Also the next day your kimono made of your chosen fabric was ready. −WCS

Have been working with a group of executives in charge of setting up the nylon plants and had them in hysterics when I announced I would call them by a special group name "The Seven Samurai" (there are seven of them), only condition: I was to be a special member—"Western style" . . . As close as possible I have the boys in hysterics by announcing each meeting with the phrase that "this meeting of the Seven Samurai will now come to order." Someone overheard me tell Mr. Muto, "take it easy, Mr. M., you work too hard"—this was also considered a humorous and bold statement to the President. Much laughter.

Meanwhile the Kanebo Cosmetics climb had been started. Today I went through two meetings and will finish with nylon tomorrow and Wednesday. On Thursday or Friday I go to Tokyo for Cosmetics. I hope to be able to get away at the end of the week.

Having watched you use that Botany cream, I am an expert on cosmetics and will probably come up with more ideas than Revlon ever had. One thing I will do is stress the spending of money. Oh! Yes, on the men's side I was surprised when they told me that men's toiletries are a big thing in Japan. Evidently my dear mother was wrong when she chided my father for using face-cream—the Samurai do it! She said only sissies use cream. Am enclosing a box-top of a sample Kanebo cosmetics for men. If you notice it carries the slogan "Secret of Beauty—Creams Come True," which I thought up about six months ago. When they proudly showed me the same slogan on their complete line of men's cosmetics, I told them it was meant only for the Women's cosmetics. But like my dear mother, they insisted that "men" too like to be beautiful—so I stopped arguing with them. I am the official slogan maker.

Dior in Japan

Stemming out of the idea of licensing famous brand names came the idea of Christian Dior for Kanebo.

I had been friendly for a number of years with Christian Dior in Paris and New York, through my relationship with M.J. Rouet, Managing Director. I had known Christian Dior and after his death I kept up a small acquaintance with M. Marcel Boussac, the owner of Christian Dior enterprises, and was well acquainted with its operations. The first idea was conceived at the Drake. I was having breakfast with Mr. Rouet, and suddenly the idea occurred to me that Mr. Rouet would be interested to shake hands with Kanebo, so I telephoned Mr. Muto, who at the time used to come to New York rather frequently, and he agreed it was a good idea. Mr. Muto was in fact very open to the idea. I went back to Paris and renewed my early license discussion with Mr. Rouet. I had been involved with other business affairs in the United States with Mr. Rouet and knew pretty well of their technical procedures and operations. He voiced the view that modern communications are quickly breaking down barriers between different people and said that Fashion is international and "knows no boundaries." Highlights of the Dior visit were a series of fashion shows, press, radio and television interviews in the leading cities. It was attended by members of the Imperial family, the French Ambassador and a cross-section of high ranking diplomatic and social figures in Tokyo. The Dior creations by Bohan scored an immediate hit.

Welcoming Dior. Mr. Muto and Madame Asabuki. (She was a great translator of French literature and came from a most distinguished family).

Mr. and Mrs. Muto introducing Bohan and de Poix to the Princess.

Marc Bohan inspecting fabrics.

WCS and Muto. First Dior fashion show in Tokyo.

115

Art Gallery Going at Yamanaka, Kyoto

I purchased this Tang Buddha head (at Kan Art Museum at that time). In the back, 2 dogs which I also purchased.

Mr. Muto is an art connoisseur—
He really is.

While Mr. Muto was extremely busy, he would always have time to go to art dealers and museums and to speak about the world of art. He was an expert at appraising Chinese and Japanese art. Very often Mr. Muto and I would be discussing art in his office, while outside his executives would wait patiently, probably wondering what important business affairs we were discussing.

—WCS

Tea Party at Mr. Saito's with Mr. Muto and the Segal family

Saito, Cora, Margaret

He would ask me, "What do you think of this Sung piece?"

Saito family

Mr. Saito was one of the most important art dealers of Japan, dealing almost entirely with Japanese art. Many of his clients, among the nobility of Japan, would visit him in his gallery and home in Kita Kamakura as he had access to the most important treasures of Japan. Mr. Muto was one of his clients and several pieces from my own collection came to me through Mr. Saito. He was a friend of Dr. Suzuki and Asahina Roshi. He never dressed in Western clothes, had his own tea house in the garden of his home. He invited Mr. Muto and my family to a tea party.

—WCS

117

Visit to Dr. Suzuki in Kita Kamakura

Dr. Suzuki with Mihoko Okamura

Spent a wonderful day with Dr. Suzuki. Will write you at length from Osaka. Wish to get this to you before I leave at 6:00 a.m. to Murai. As I write, Muto is going to Persia and I corrected the English speech he is preparing for the Shah.

Dr. Suzuki's 90th birthday will be held in Kyoto, and I will try to get McArthur there. He should represent the U.S.A. In the middle of our talk in the garden, Suzuki comes out with, "Mr. Segal, how is BEAUTY?" He really remembers that little girl. He has his own cat—very nice, but not in Beauty's class!. . . As I only had one day in Tokyo before I had to leave for Osaka, I called Mihoko and arranged to spend Tuesday with Dr. Suzuki. I was supposed to arrive in Kita Kamakura where he lives at almost 11:30 in the morning. But as I got up very early, I figured I would pay a visit to Asahina at Engakuji. I got there at ten, and had a strange feeling of the quietness and special atmosphere of the place. After I walked around I asked the two monks stationed there to tell Asahina that, if possible, I would like to see him. Unfortunately, he was in Tokyo, so I left my card, and after more walking and going into some of the old buildings, I made my way to the high hill where Suzuki lives. There was a great deal of construction going on, and it is quite a climb. Imagine the dismay when, in broken Japanese, a maid said Mihoko and he were waiting for me at the Kita Kamakura station. I rushed down there, and there they were, very much concerned too, because the train had arrived, but not me.

I felt really terrible to think of the old man climbing up and down a steep hill for no reason. But he looked fine and so did Mihoko, who is thinner and even prettier than before. After greetings and inquiries about you, we took a short walk to a wonderful old house, and seated facing a lovely garden, we began to eat, drink and talk.

For a ninety-year old man he drank quite a bit of hot sake, although he ate very sparingly. Some of the things he said which I could remember, I am writing. But as you know, my memory is poor except when my eyes are shut. And as usual, one has to keep one's eyes open with Suzuki.

"Zazen sitting is necessary because by sitting (he meant meditation of course), a sort of sedimentation of elements takes place which permits Satori, opens one to another experience of oneself.

"By sitting, enough concentration can be developed to prevent thoughts disturbing contact with oneself, both thoughts from without and impulses that distract from within.

"Some people come quicker than others to this Satori." He said that is like with artists. "Some people are born with more of a flair for it than others, but it is always waiting if one holds attention long and strong enough.

"People," he emphasized, "are different. They need different approaches. That is why one man will work better with one master than another." He didn't elaborate on this except to say that one way may not be suited to all people.

"When you talk about it (satori), it isn't there."

He spoke a great deal about Bodidharma—how he was not really understood by many of his followers. And that as a foreigner he was startlingly different from the Chinese and Japanese, but that he was a most inspiring and original teacher—and that he had a number of strong Indian disciples who also impressed the Chinese and Japanese of those times.

He spoke also about the Garden of Eden relating it to an "Innocence" from an inside place within man - how we make a thing beautiful, ugly, etc. (Opposites).

He joked about our sake drinking—said he has some friends who are older than he is and actually live only on Sake—no eating of solid food.

Once in a while he would answer my own second-hand thoughts by saying, "Not bad, Mr. Segal."

Oil portrait of Mihoko by WCS

It was something to see that old man climb back up the hill at a pace that left me really out of breath. He seemed very strong, but I noticed that Mihoko guides his elbow every once in a while, as if his sight is poor.

We talked till about five . . . saw the new library which he said he hoped would be of use to people after he dies. They will finish building it in a few more months and it is quite a job. Set against a bamboo forest—two story concrete fireproof building. When I asked Mihoko where the money came from, she said it was in a strange way. If you remember the Japanese man, Hidemitsu, who called me on his visit to the U.S. and wished us to have tea at the Pierre Hotel? He is an ardent lover of the XIXth Century Japanese artist called Sengai (that's why Suzuki gave him my name—I evidently had the same approach and enthusiasm for Sengai's work as Hidemitsu.) He is an old man too, and he and Dr. Suzuki also have Sengai's art in common. When Hidemitsu found out that Suzuki wanted a memorial library of stone to house his books, he simply gave him the money. He is not a Zen Buddhist—just wanted Suzuki to have the building, and as he is head of Japan's biggest oil company, he gives whatever is needed. A good friend! Mihoko, however, does all the work with architects, builders, etc. (They had to build a special railroad track to haul the material up the hill— and the crew of builders live in a specially built house right on the job.) She has matured well, except she can see no one else but Suzuki, and lets a little sharp criticism in her voice when speaking of many of his visitors from all over the world. She also acts as interpreter when professors visit Asahina at Engakuji nearby.

Mihoko is really indispensable to Suzuki. He writes, she told me, almost all of the time. But he scribbles on any scrap and envelope that comes to hand. She has to read his difficult writing, and then type it and put it in the right place. She thinks Asahina is also a great teacher. About Watts, when his name came up—she cracked something about he is "outside Zen" only.

When I got off the train at Osaka "they" gave me a big welcome. About ten men to greet me - but I was rushed to the Kanomori, and before I could wash up, I was rushed again to Yodogawa for a meeting with the directors. It was tough going, as I was not too well prepared. Today I had a meeting with rather large groups which went well. But I think with Muto out of the country (he is acting as special ambassador to Iran) they feel free to make me work hard. They are really scared of him. After the last meeting I called Mrs. Sasaki - and she was all sweetness and charm - when would we have dinner? When could they expect me? I explained the position, and will try to make it next week.

I have to prepare to tell a group of technical engineers about the oxidation process which the Hoechst Co. of Germany is using in their fiber operations. That will be good. Ah! So!

Rinzai - Han Do

Going back to Zazen. You will recall Suzuki trying to explain the feeling mu in the pit of the stomach. Evidently your silent ten strokes are made right to the lower stomach. You stop for a while as you have collected some attention by the physical placing of something in your lower part. Then you repeat for further concentration. From then on you concentrate on "NOTHING" as an idea wishing for "NOTHING" but always holding on to the posture and keeping firm but soft. Otherwise the stick. After a while, something comes. It is a question, of course, like Ouspensky said, "Depth and duration." They go for both twice a day - and don't leave it to the meetings to do it haphazardly. So they schedule their self-remembering and even supervise it and in groups for a long time.

All this may make no sense in writing but in this wonderful atmosphere it seems to work. I will try to explain it better when I get home.

At the Daitokuji, Sasaki Zendo

Coming directly from Osaka, where we had our usual business sessions, I arrived at Mrs. Sasaki's in time to have dessert and coffee with her and the ever-present Waskins-San. She was very gay and unreserved and we chatted away for about a half-hour. Then it was time to commence the Zazen sitting. Tonight she told me she would not sit as she was going to a meeting later on and wished to prepare her material. We only sat for an hour and it seemed very short. The quiet atmosphere is not usual in big cities.

Then we left the hall and went into her house and there she dressed in monk's robes in front of a little desk. There were about fourteen others present, including one Zen monk and two other Japanese. Also beside the monk a young math teacher from Wesleyan, a chap by the name of Clarke, who, when I came in, leaned over and whispered "Are you going to put out a Zen issue of *American Fabrics*, Mr. Segal?"

Mrs. Sasaki started the talk by saying that the Zen monk would lead us in sutra chanting. Evidently she runs a prep school for Zen as she said they would have to be able to know the sutras when they go off to a Japanese monastery. I chanted along (probably off key) and it was rather pleasant, a steady rhythm, which was maintained unbroken for almost ten minutes. Then she started to speak and almost at the beginning, I was startled to hear about "Mr. Segal, who is here with us and who everybody knows has a wonderful old cat named Beauty." I must have missed something because evidently Beauty figured into what she was going to talk about, but I couldn't make the connection. Her main theme was that the student must know something about (1) pre-Buddhist cosmology; (2) the history of the early Buddhist hermits and teachers; (3) understand how and why zazen is of fundamental importance in their search. Her descriptions of the pre-Buddhists' understanding of time and space as applied to cosmology was very close to modern astrophysics and of course to the ray of creation concepts. According to her sources we are—in time—just at the beginning of the worst period in the earth's history. We are in the 7000th year of a bad spell that will last another 450,000 years.

Our conversation when we were at dinner earlier was mainly about the six ways of meditation: (1) sitting (2) walking (3) lying down (4) looking at tops of trees (5) breathing (6) she forgot what it was!

Of course there was always, at Kanebo, a car and chauffeur ready for me whenever I wished to go, and quite frequently I would leave early in the evening for a dinner date with Ruth Fuller Sasaki, in Kyoto. She had marvelous dinners, homemade coffee ice cream with meringues. She surely lived well for a Zen priest. At that time she told me she was sixty-eight. This seemed terribly old, yet she never missed a meditation and she seemed to work harder than any of the young men.

Sasaki says Central Asia is still full of monasteries. That current excavation in Central China and Asia deserts also show numerous ancient places where many monasteries are being found. She described the period of Emperor Asoka, about 800 B.C. She says there are people with phenomenal memories still existing today in Nepal, Burma and India who can quote 1000 pages of ancient scriptures by memory. Modern scholars can call on these men for their memory.

On Attention

Mrs. Sasaki agreed that it is a lack of mind concentration that holds students back and that meditation faces them with the problem of strengthening their attention and seeing that their attention is weak.

At this point they were sitting from seven in the morning to nine in the evening, with five minutes to stretch their legs and a half hour breakfast period.

It was just like the typical Japanese monasteries sitting at her place. There were about fourteen people sitting, half of them foreigners. They, too, had the man with the stick.

She herself told me how she used to sit fourteen or fifteen hours a day over a several week period. One week period she sat for twenty-three hours a day, with one hour for sleeping. She said it was a wonderful experience, and not as hard or as difficult as it sounds.

She described very poetically her feelings when sitting one night, with the snow falling.

Mrs. Sazaki on Zazen

When she got on the subject of Zazen, she was good. The mind that is out of control is the big obstacle. So, sitting is the beginning of control. When one keeps the body still, it is like water that can gradually clear itself, with things settling and eventually a deeper thought process begins to take place. The sitting position in Zazen is important physiologically and psychologically. A real lotus position insures that the body will not distract the attention. It puts the man in a position to effectively collect himself. She spoke about the double triangle, which involves the shoulders and legs.

Attention—sensing is in the stomach—and the rhythm as she demonstrated it was not at all easy to maintain. This Zen breathing, she affirmed, was very valuable in achieving mind control. It acted on the sympathetic nervous system rather than brain-nervous system and unnecessary, uncontrollable thoughts were slowed down. She again used the expression: "You don't breath, you are being breathed." This ability to be breathed instead of breathing gives very fine results.

Visiting Dr. Suzuki Again— Kamakura, Four Years On

Suzuki at 94 looks better than he did ten years ago and aside from his hearing, he seems sharper than ever.

<u>About people</u>
<u>Blythe the author</u>: I received the impression from

Suzuki's indirect remarks that Blythe never penetrated to the fullest depths of Zen and this resulted in a rather frustrated state in the last year of his life. He was essentially a poet – and perhaps his difficulty was in equating Zen and poetry. Seemed Blythe lacked the training of discipline (I'm not sure).

Merton – the Trappist Monk: Suzuki began by saying it would be worth my while to go to Kentucky to visit and talk with a monk in a monastery. I didn't connect the name for a while. But later, I realized it was the writer. He came to visit Suzuki last year in New York and Suzuki said he was one of the most unusual men he ever spoke with. He said he was close to the real Buddhism as all real Buddhists are close to real Christianity and kept harping away at arranging a meeting.

Alan Watts: Suzuki took apart the idea of L.S.D. and Mescaline from the standpoint that consciousness stems directly from God in what we know of God – and while L.S.D. is also part of God it is only a small part and the effects – which people take as a reflection of concsciousness – is not cosmic or God-consciousness. He took exception to Watts use and advocacy of drugs, saying that these later prevent cognition of the real thing.

Also he received a visit recently from Terence Grey (Wei Wu Wei) but said that Grey did not speak at all. At this point Mihoko added, Wei Wu Wei's wife (Grey's wife) was more interesting than he.

We spoke about Chinese texts. He said they are translating many cases of old Chinese texts. I asked him: why do Zen people write and talk so much if they are against writing and talking? His reply was that as long as people ask questions and think they must have answers, the writing and talking must be done. But he quite agreed about the fact that the world contains three billion Buddhas, who think they are men and women and who go on suffering, enjoying themselves, questioning, etc. without knowing who they are. Also expression helps people.

He remembered so much of our Chester visit; Beauty the cat and of course, you. I told him about Elizabeth and her writings and Mihoko burst in that Liz in her talent takes after you.

Visiting Soen with Madame de Salzmann and Friends

Soen was recuperating when we arrived at Ryutakuji with Madame de Salzmann and company. I recall we gathered in his little study, reached by a small flight of steps. Almost immediately, Soen challenged us with a kind of koan: "Find the Buddha statue in this room." There was no Buddha statue, as far as we could see.

After a hard journey, it had been raining, our cars were stuck in the mud . . . we were a little puzzled. Where is the Buddha in the room? Soen made it clear it was a statue . . . ? After a few minutes silence, no one had the answer. I was the go-between, having brought my friends. I had to be inspired, and had to make my teacher look good. My hand reached out to a piece of rock, the size of a man's fist, which was on the shelf behind Soen's seat. When I held it up in silence it suddenly seemed to resemble (with imagination) a figure of a small seated Buddha. Soen looked satisfied when I said, "This is the Buddha." He laughed.

It happened to be Soen's mother's birthday which I understood he always celebrated. We arranged to meet before dawn in a special room where the statue, a woodcarving of a former Master was. I believe it might have been Hakuin.

Also at the occasion were two musicians with whom Soen had arranged to come from a far-off part of Japan to play. It was an eerie morning. First of all, he slowly opened the door in the dark. I was astonished at the life-like, impressive appearance of the carving. Then, the emotion with which Soen performed the ceremony in honor of his mother's memory and still further, the weird mystical beauty of the lute in the dim morning light.

I think of Japan with nostalgia. Our
trip will bear some consequences — It was
an important thing to be done —
Bill has been the best help and friend
one could imagine —

Photo of Dr. Suzuki a few weeks before his death, at Kita Kamakura. At his left Madame de Salzmann. At his right Dr. de Salzmann. Cora is shown between Dr. Vaysse, who wrote an interesting book on Gurdjieff, and myself. At this visit Dr. Suzuki was in very good form. We were having tea, and to illustrate a point, he threw a cat at me, and said, "here, Mr. Segal" . . . what was interesting, of course, was to see a 96 year old man in enough possession of his physical power, to quickly reach down, pick up a cat, and throw it accurately into my arms.

—WCS

I have sent In search of the miraculous
to Kabori with a letter and have
written also and sent the book to
Asahina and Myoko — To Wm Sasaki
I gave it when she was sick in Paris —
So, the relation with Japan is kept
alive — I have asked Myoko to let
me know when Dr Suzuki will go to
Italy and I certainly will see him there.
There is something precious in the relation
which have been established there. It
can lead to something important and
I will remain quite open to it. —
you see what you have done !—

                    J. de S.

We stayed at the temple four or five days. It was the cold season. All were freezing except Madame de Salzmann (who had a big fur coat). Madame de Salzmann and I got up early, at 4:00 A.M., with Soen. But he was incapacitated. He had fallen in the mountains. However, he conducted the ceremony. He moved with caution, care and grace. Soen was a famous poet and an artist. Madame de Salzmann later often spoke on how impressive she found Roshi Soen; the presence of his movements—when he was suffering a great deal of pain.

Every six months the monks went out to a big dinner, given by a rich local farmer. I recall the preparation as the monks assembled to march the three miles from the Temple to the farmer's compound. Soen had all the monks lined up in a military fashion before starting. Several had drums to beat the rhythm of the march. Soen insisted that I would be dressed in hakame (split trousers) for walking more easily. We made quite a sight as we marched across the countryside. We performed a ceremony at the farm, and said prayers for the welfare of the family.

Then came the dinner . . . what a dinner! Course after course lavishly served with large bowls of hot sake. I remember those young men who had been on a very rigid diet for months. It was natural that eating and drinking took on astonishing proportions. By the time we had to leave, saying prayers at the end of the ceremony, most of the monks were drunk. I recall my own enthusiastic reciting of the prayers and sutras (though I knew not much of what I was saying).

And the journey back home in the moonlight—like a picture of Kurosawa; the lanterns, the drums, the chanting.

Soen always thought New York was a mountain. On the nineteenth floor of our apartment he used to say, "We are on the roof of the world." Soen Nakagawa (master of Taisan Roshi Shimaro, New York) was the abbot of the Renzai Zen Monastery, Ryutakuji, in Mishima City. He was a great artist, and had charge of many paintings of Hakuin. He brought these out to us, to look at them. I had known him from previous trips, the first time with Reps.

On one summer trip Soen and I arranged to get up early, for a number of days, before the 3:30 A.M. awakening time. We'd go out for long walks in the early dawn. One time, after the sun had risen, we walked a long way, and saw a beautiful persimmon tree (khakis). Soen suggested we eat some of the fruits. I offered to climb up, figuring I was in better shape. When I came down with several persimmons which we ate with gusto, he said, "I give you a new name, Seru-san. Mr. Monkey, you are such a good climber." When we would wake up in the morning, as we passed sleeping quarters of the young monks, he gestured, "Look at them . . . all sleeping Buddhas . . . but they don't know it."

Once he gave me yellow apples to offer Dr. Suzuki...I remember Dr. Suzuki making his remark, "Soen is too strict with the young men. Now young men are not like in the Middle Ages . . . they are not as strong." Dr. Suzuki thought it was not good for the health of these monks to go through so much hardship.

Letter to Madame de Salzmann

September 4, 1970

Dear Madame

I feel I should write to you about the strangest, most unexpected visit which I received from Soen Nakagawa Roshi and Tai-san. (You remember Soen is Roshi of Ryutakuji, which we visited in Japan, and Tai-san is the head of the New York Zen Society we visited on 68th Street.) The bell rang at the door of my New York apartment, and suddenly there were two strange figures—shaved heads, monks robes and all. I was so astonished it probably showed in my face. Seeing my startled expression, Soen grabbed my two hands and exclaimed, "It's like a dream." He kept repeating the word, dream, dream, dream.

So there we were, the three of us. They had not heard about Cora. When I told them, Soen proposed that we have a drink for her as well as for you as our absent companion in commemoration of our visit four years ago, so we placed glasses for the absent ones, and poured a few drops of brandy in each glass, as they said for the taste of the tongue in it. Then we had a five minute silence. Later on another silence and still later, the two chanted a service for Cora's journey. It was certainly all very strange.

We talked about what they were doing. They have just finished with a week's Shesshin in Connecticut and will start another, two weeks from now. They said that about 50 people are coming from different parts of the U.S. When I half jokingly suggested that I might come, they enthusiastically agreed. When I told them that I could not make it for the week, too much to do here, Soen suggested that I come for a day, or when I wanted, but looking at Tai-san's face, I felt he was not too enthusiastic about breaking in, in the middle of the event. Soen also noticed his expression and he began to kid him about his slavishness to rules.

Soen looked fine—far healthier looking than when we saw him in Japan. He is also going to Hawaii for a week to give a Shesshin there. They have a zendo on one of the Hawaiian islands. He said I should write to Reps and have him get in touch in Hawaii. Then he said that although Reps is older than I, I am his older brother. Reps probably leads a healthier life than I do and so I think he looks younger. Soen evidently fell in love with the English word "dream," and kept repeating that life and dream were the same and interchangeable. Perhaps he was only trying to cheer me up a little.

I told him I was going on a trip to India, and he said it was fine to do that, and I would find what is true where I go. (I did not tell him I was going with you.) All in all, it was a most exhilarating evening, perhaps because so unexpected. I will probably pay them a visit at the 68th Street Zendo, as he will be in

New York for a few days.

It was interesting to see them together. He is obviously Tai-san's teacher, but the latter impressed me as having a great deal.

I asked them how the American Zen Shesshin goes. He said that while they devote a great deal of time to meditation, they also do work on the grounds, that meals take time, and that Soen gives a lecture each day. He speaks English much better than I thought he did. The younger man speaks English extremely well. Evidently they travel together and hold quite a number of these intensive, one week periods. When I remarked that it must be hard work, Soen said no— it's a rest and very refreshing for him. I must say that they look very well and rested. Maybe we should take them to Armonk and tire them out a little.

On the trip side, I have sent a letter to the Afghanistan Ambassador to France asking that he meet me in Paris. I just dispatched it so it will probably be some time before I hear from him.

I have some other good names for Kabul, including the American Embassy. And a friend strongly urges that we spend at least two or three days in Ispahan. I think the hotel to reserve is the Shah Abbas.

Letter from Madame de Salzmann

22 September, 1970

Dear Bill,

Enjoyed your letter and the description of the meditation of the zendo in New York. It is true that a participation to a rite has a very strong effect on one, also because of the feeling of togetherness, of fulfilling a task beyond one's egoist subjectivity—I remember very well the dignified, religious way Soen Roshi led the ceremony in Japanese and it is true that he is an artist, a kind of poet.

H.H. circa 1970

India:

Travels to Dharamsala, 1970–1971

"The robe of Zen reached only to the knees, but that of Tibetan Buddhism covered everything right down to the feet." —H.H. the Dalai Lama

After the death of his wife, Cora, Bill took two trips to India accompanying Madame de Salzmann. Very special conditions had been arranged for him by Canada's High Commissioner to India, James George, including a trip to Dharamsala to meet His Holiness the Dalai Lama. Going through the mountains, Bill was accompanied by a distinguished guide-interpreter, Lobsang Lhalungpa, son of the last State Oracle of Tibet. To his astonishment Bill saw His Holiness and Lhalungpa embrace warmly as they met. They were great friends. Some years later in America Lhalungpa made a new translation of Milarepa's life. We were very familiar with the Tibetan saint. During our long evenings in our country home we often read aloud from the 100,000 Songs of Milarepa. Like the sculptor, Brancusi, who had on his night table Milarepa's Namthar, Bill kept next to his bed the Jetsun biography by Evans-Wentz. Bill visited several great Rinpoches in Darjeeling–Dudjom Rinpoche, head of the Nyingmapa school, Chatral Rinpoche, Kanjur Rinpoche, Gyurtala Rinpoche. He met many Tibetan masters at the Canadian Embassy through his friend, James George. During these trips to India Bill wrote me many letters.

October 25, 1970
We left Paris on Air France and had a fine flight to Rome. At the Rome airport we were delayed two hours (1) because of a very rigid security check against hijackers (how they could think Madame de Salzmann was a hijacker I don't know) (2) because of a violent storm.

A rather long, hard non-stop flight to arrive at Delhi airport at four in the morning. But the Canadian

Ambassador in person (with wife and staff) were there having made all the necessary arrangements. So off we went to the embassy where we are now. Very, very comfortable living but rather removed from the turmoil of India.

The staff, I was told, numbers about one hundred, most of them devoted to taking care of four people. So you can see that I was living an unaccustomed life of luxury—ultra. My scant wardrobe is washed, cleaned, repaired etc on the hour. Attendants are silent, unobtrusive and seem to anticipate every possible personal need.

We were rather tired the first day, but I went off to the market place, mosques etc. to get a feel for the city.

It is quite a place, with humanity (as far as numbers go) very plentiful. The poverty is endemic but the people seem to be relaxed and more or less enjoying themselves on the pitifully small material means that they have.

After dinner we went to a dance recital with one of the foreign ministers and were more or less guests of India. You know the stuff, photographers, flowers, etc. I think I was painted as the Ambassador from Iran and accordingly shook hands with many people. The recital was wonderful and I was struck by the chief dancer who I think would be a great success in the U.S. and Europe. She had a great charm besides her technical ability. I also like the music and the general presentation. Oh yes, during the day while wandering about the old city I was accosted by a fortune teller who appeared out of a wall; grabbed my hand and told me how lucky I was etc., etc.

The journey is just beginning and it would be too early to write about the temple, religious people, etc. But I hope to do so.

I hope you are well and that when you arrived home all was well. I was very grateful to be with you, after all! Things are happening so fast—(we are off to the borders of Tibet tomorrow) that I haven't had much time to miss the West. But I suppose that I will soon be wishing to be with people who are close to me. Tomorrow we are off on another trek, first to see Sai Baba whom some people think is the new incarnated god—and then to Himalayan Lamas—looking forward to both. This morning we watched India's great dancer Yamini Krishnamurti at her practice in her Delhi house. Her father sits with her like a dragon watching a princess. She is really marvelous—like a gupta female goddess come to life. But when she stops dancing she becomes a rather ordinary looking Indian woman. She had six musicians at her practice and I made a recording of the music. Delhi is very hot but like all truly Oriental cities it is very colorful and alive and I have enjoyed walking through the bazaars.

April 15, 1971

Just a word to tell that we saw Sai Baba yesterday and it was quite a thing. Although many of his followers assured us that he was descended from above (so are you, I and everybody) it is hard to accept. But in any case I made a film of him and you will see for yourself. We stayed in Madras until this morning, traveling in a day or two we start for the Kingdom of Sikhim which is next to Bhutan and Nepal and on the Tibetan-Chinese border.

We are just waiting for the papers as it is difficult to travel. We will probably stay in the Palace and in any case expect to see something new.

It is very hot so we stay close to the Embassy. The daughter of the house gave us a recital of Indian Dances also. Quite interesting. Will probably show you the film I made. "Probably" because it may not come out.

As you may guess it is quite luxurious where we are—but totally sealed off from the reality of India. When we start traveling it will be different.

Japan

After 1970

Some time after our marriage, Bill felt a strong desire to go back to Japan so that his ties would not be cut because of the accident. He had been deeply touched by the reaction of Mr. Junji Itoh, the second president of Kanebo, who had always considered Bill a sensi and had become a friend. Bill received a hand-written letter from Mr. Itoh, giving him a contract in which he was assured, in elegant terms, that henceforth, no matter what he undertook to do or not do, the contract would remain in force indefinitely. Mr. Itoh then created an interesting international gathering which Bill chaired each year for a number of years. Senior executives from various departments of Kanebo would assemble from around the world to spend a week together looking ahead and giving the company advice on future policy. I had the privilege of being the only woman participant in this "advisory group" which met in Tokyo or New York or Paris.

Bill would invariably begin each session with a silent meditation. The projects he would present were always audacious and usually too avant garde to be adopted by the hide-bound traditionalist corporation Kanebo had become by the end of the century.

WCS and MBS visiting Mr. Itoh

Bringing Japanese artwork back to Japan

WCS and Mr. Itoh

Advisory group in New York

Imperial reception room. First visit after WCS's accident. *Left to right*: Mr. Itoh, Mr. Fukunaka, WCS, MBS, Mr. Sano

An Exhibition by William Segal
Fifty Years of American Painting
ウイリアム・シーガル「アメリカ絵画50年」

In the 80s and 90s our trips to Japan continued in the "double life" manner established in 1952—business, work, and seminars in Osaka were punctuated by most refined dinners with Mr. Itoh's family. And serveral days were spent in Kyoto with our elegant friend Nanrei Kobori, abbott at the Daitoku-ji monastery.

In 1992 Kanebo sponsored a retrospective exhibit of Bill's paintings, which Mr. Itoh very successfully organized in Tokyo.

I I have a
different face

The Accident

"Lucky man. One accident like yours is worth ten thousand sittings in a monastery!"

–Soen Nakagawa Roshi, abbot of Ryutakuji

June 9, 1971

It was a summer afternoon. I had left my New York office and was on my way to Fire Island to see my daughter. It was hot and I'd had a substantial lunch and a couple of drinks. I was feeling sleepy. I was, as usual, driving fast.

My last recollection before the accident is of a familiar stretch of road, a few miles from my destination. I must have fallen asleep at the wheel. I found out later that the car had crashed at full speed into the stone abutment of one of the overpass bridges.

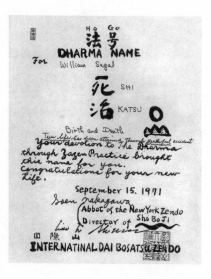

I came to, briefly, while they were taking me out of the wreck. There was tremendous pain in my legs and hips and I remember saying to the men working to extricate me, "Be careful, for God's sake, be careful . . ." Then I blacked out again.

The next impression was total darkness lit up by two round disks - like two suns. At that moment I thought, as I remember, that I was either dreaming or dead. Then I had a very pleasant feeling as if I was gently being moved towards the left-hand sun. With this came the additional feeling that if I let myself go towards the left, I would surely die. It was easy and all very soothingly happening (I was following all this from some part of myself).

At this moment I knew that I could either live if I wished to undertake burden of suffering or I could die gently and peacefully. At the same moment, I also had what could be called a seizure, of considering. I knew that if I died, people would say that I had planned it, to die just about a year after Cora's death, in the same locality and most likely my body would be resting in the same hospital. It was, or it would appear too staged an accident.

I don't remember anything after that except that I heard, in one of my brief moments of consciousness, someone say, "Well, we've given him the last rites." My daughter's name sounds Irish and must have made them think I was Catholic. They had called in a priest to give me the last rites.

Four or five days later, when I regained consciousness, I learned that I had been taken to the nearest hospital where a team of doctors was assembled to try to save my life. Both my hips were shattered and I had a fractured skull. My face was crushed to the point of what is called "Le Forte injuries number three," total separation of all the facial bones from the skull, as bad as it can get. All the bones were broken. That's why my face is completely changed.

Every part of me seemed crushed. My first clear recollections were of the feeling of being wired together—tubes everywhere, my face, my penis, arms and legs. The pain was unremitting. I couldn't urinate. I couldn't breathe. I couldn't see. I was practically blind and deaf. I had a vague understanding of what was going on around me. It was like being in a dark cave with only a dim light. Once in a while I'd wake up to a faint glimmer and the murmur of voices.

I said to myself "Either I am going to die or I'm not going to die. It's all right. In either case I want to watch—to see what goes on." I dedicated myself entirely to seeing what was happening to my body, to me.

Let me give an example of how that worked. One of the doctors came to my room some days after I'd gone through an operation they had hoped would help repair my hip. He said, "I'm afraid this time is no better than the last; it didn't take. We'd like to try again. Are you up to it tomorrow?" My first thought was, "All that pain again? NO." I had faced one outrage to my body after another and there was no end in sight. All the same I said "Well, O.K., let's do it. O.K., O.K." My attitude was— accept everything: pain, relief from pain, living, dying. Don't hinder anything. If I lived, I lived. If I died, I died. All my attention, all my passion, was for watching.

This attitude of course had disadvantages. For example, when I was waiting on a gurney outside the operating room, before they gave me the anesthetic, I would get cold. A hospital corridor can be drafty and even though it was summer I was often intensely cold. By this time I had lost thirty or forty pounds because I was unable to eat, and I was rather wasted away. Hospitals don't seem to take into account the sensitivity of the patient to small drafts that wouldn't bother a person in good health. The sensible thing would have been to ask for blankets or ask to be moved to a warmer place. But I didn't wish to risk making exceptions to this attitude of just watching. I would say to myself, "Let it go. It's a small thing to endure the cold for a few minutes."

WCS and Cora Segal

I knew also that I was going to have to be operated on many, many times and I could only get through it if I disciplined my thought to take one hurdle at a time. I'd tell myself, "They're just going to shore up my cheekbone; that's not so bad." I concentrated entirely on what was actually taking place or about to take place. I took one hurdle at a time and didn't think about the future.

The doctors were surprised that I lived. They told me later, "We didn't think you'd survive the first few days. Then we were ready to leave you permanently crippled; at least we would have resurrected half of you. We kept operating only because you were able to go on."

The breathing tube in my throat made this an especially bad period. They were trying to repair my face. My nose had been smashed and breathing was a serious problem. Still, I would forget about myself when I thought of all the courageous people throughout the hospital. The man next to me was dying without a murmur.

My wife had just died a few months before and I was dependent on my two daughters more than on anyone else. One of my daughters was on her way to visit me. She was coming with my sister-in-law in a car with a driver. On the way there was an accident. The driver wasn't hurt but my sister-in-law was killed instantly and my daughter's neck was broken. She was taken to a hospital near mine. I could only think about her, stretched out, unable to move, unable to talk. The shock of hearing of her accident marked a new phase for me; I passed beyond my own troubles. She recovered and is alright today.

In the hospital, I came to an attitude of appreciation for the smallest things. My jaws had been wired to my skull and when they were sufficiently released so that I could manage to suck through a straw, I was overwhelmed with gratitude. It was my first non-intravenous nourishment. The sensation of a fluid going down my throat filled me with gratitude. The nuance in the taste of banana-flavored milk drink was remarkable even though I'd never particularly cared for bananas or milk.

There is a beauty in the everyday lives of people. I would watch the man who cleaned at night and sometimes we exchanged a few words. He was a recent immigrant who had taken the only job he could get. How carefully and conscientiously he worked. How economical his movements were. There was in every gesture the nobility of doing what life required of him.

It was touching to see that the girl who mixed the mild drink wanted to get it exactly to my taste. She cared very much that it have just the right amount of sweetness.

The first time I was able to be taken for a ride in a wheelchair it was a big adventure. What joy when the nurse wheeled me in the corridor and I could look around and see people! In the Intensive Care Unit and in my room I had seen only one or two people at a time. Every face, every doorway was a revelation, as if I were newly born or seeing it on a new planet. Everything was an event. The motion of the wheelchair was a sensory delight.

One takes everything for granted until it's taken away. If one has a relatively good body and mind, one is proud of "my" strength and "my" intelligence though they are simply given. It doesn't take much, one small blow; they're gone, and I'm not so great. Whatever could be taken away so easily couldn't have belonged to me. It all added up to a humbling, chastening experience. Best of all, it brought a new level of tolerance in my attitude toward others.

When we're helpless we're more sensitive to the existing but hidden conditions that govern our lives. Ordinarily we're not responsive to invisible forces. Suddenly – they exist.

A great letting-go is required when one is ill. Let the body relax. Go to sleep. Go to sleep. Nature is speaking and you need to listen. Go to sleep. Don't try too much. Just sleep. Listen and obey. Underneath, the healing process must be related to patience. Wait. Let go. Let another force take over. You're not going to do anything anyway. The more you push the worse it is. So: acceptance. Acceptance of what happens, whatever happens, even death.

Although I often felt I wanted to die, I wasn't drawn toward death only because it meant release from suffering. I was half-way there; it would have been so easy. Coming back required that I gather myself together and sometimes I felt I could not summon the energy.

It's hard to be certain about something as central as will. I remember one of the last operations, a couple of years later. They were taking some wires out of my jaw. I was in fairly good physical condition by that time but it seemed to me that my will was weaker. I thought the will had been trained, so to speak, by exercise, but there was very little of it. It was as if there is a finite quantity of will and my supply had been diminished by all the previous demands on it or it may be that will comes forward to champion life only when life is seriously challenged. In the case of this operation, perhaps I was in no real danger and the will slumbered in peace. I don't know. I'm not so sure of myself, of my so-called will. The prospect of more surgery fills me with trepidation.

I still don't know what to make of a certain strange occurrence. A friend of mine, an American who had many followers in an oriental type of religion, came one day and told me "Listen, I've asked all my people to pray for you. Starting tonight there will be five hundred people who are going to direct their thoughts toward you to help you." I liked him very much personally but I had never agreed with his ideas. I was skeptical about being helped by distant vibrations and it must have showed in my eyes because he became more emphatic. "They will all be praying for you. You'll see, it will do you a lot of good." I didn't believe him but I was deeply touched and thanked him sincerely.

That very night, just at dawn, I saw a big white bird outside my window. Moments later it actually flew in and walked around on the window sill for at least five minutes. It was really large, as big as a pelican. In all my months in the hospital this was the first and only time I had a winged visitor. So, when my friend came to see me a few days later and asked about the result of their prayers I said "I don't know what your people did. I feel better . . . But a bird . . ." I joked about it but it's hard to know what attitude to take toward this sort of thing.

Everything is an adventure. You wonder, too, about the doctors. "What's on his mind this morning?" If he looks nervous you notice it and you try to soothe him, to calm him down.

I had nine different doctors specializing in different parts of me. They organized a team whose project at first was to keep me alive and later on was to repair me. I expected their best but realized I couldn't demand more of them than they were able to give. One doctor was quick-witted; another was slower and easy-going. One favored aggressive treatment; another was habitually conservative. Each had his individual characteristics, his strengths and limitations.

I couldn't help being interested in watching the ebb and flow of their involvement. Sometimes a physician takes a special interest in a case because it is complex and presents him with intriguing problems. Sometimes the successful resolution of a difficult case or the accomplishment of a particularly intricate surgical procedure is a trophy on his mantelpiece; the patient may be secondary. Sometimes not. Some doctors have hardly any feeling for the patient and others have a great deal of feeling. Each time a doctor walks into your room you have to look at him to see where he is; some days his mind is on his golf game.

The nurses were an on-going revelation. They run the hospital. They are always there. When they say "I'll take care of it" you can rest easy; they will.

The doctors told me to call the nurse whenever I needed medication for pain. There was a period of about three weeks in which I found myself relying on the drugs for relief when the pain became too much to bear. Then one of the doctors pointed out that I was liable to become addicted. No one had said anything about addiction before this. As soon as I heard about it I stopped all the pain shots.

You can't believe entirely in what the experts say. I was in a wheelchair for about a year. Then I went to France to see specialists there, traveling on the airplane in a wheelchair. Everyone said it was hopeless, that I'd always be a cripple although I might get by with crutches. A year later I graduated from crutches to a cane and six months after that I was able to walk without a cane. The credit belongs to a New York surgeon, one of the first doctors in the United States to use the technique of the artificial hip. He undertook an operation on my hip which other surgeons said was impossible.

I'm more or less normal now except that I have a different face.

All people who go through a serious illness probably come close to a transformation. Later, the old way reasserts itself. But another view remains underneath, bringing a degree of tolerance and understanding. One is never quite the same. Serious illness must be like a mini-death, at least a foretaste of death. Everything changes.

Once in a while, I speculate "Would I go through this experience again?" I think now, sitting in my armchair, I'd say no; I think I would rather die right away. I would not want to endure all that again. I'm older now, my body is weaker, and if I were offered a choice I'd say "Naah, let me go to sleep, the hell with it." But from another point of view, if I were wise enough to weigh the pluses and minuses, I would go through it all again.

Whether it was through his youth as an athlete at College or thanks to the practice of yoga, Bill had a complete mastery and control of his body. This care of the body showed in his conscious walking, like a Noh actor, even when, after multiple operations of the hips, his legs were of unequal length. In spite of the difficulties, he managed to walk with a grace and elegance, which seemed to me more and more remarkable.

When he had fully recovered from his accident, we went on with the publication of American Fabrics, *which not only survived but had made money since 1946. Abandoning my profession as international stylist, I learned to publish a magazine by watching my husband's astonishing power of concentration, his conception of the whole, and his ability to lay out a page, working according to the first of his four principles: Make do with what you have.*

During my University studies in France, I had always found it necessary to have more and more documentation, which paralyzed me. Bill's first principle taught me how to move.

Life in Four Places

New York

Tang Buddha

New York was home. Life in the New York apartment centered around the gray marble table where we worked and where we entertained our friends at breakfast, lunch or dinner. At one end of the table, against the wall, was the forever smiling stone Tang Buddha head, which Bill had bought thanks to Mr. Muto in Kyoto.

New York was his link with his past, through his furniture, art objects, books, the gray flannel suits, and the rare wines which his friend Jacques Rouet, director of Dior and a great connoisseur, gave him each year. The New York apartment was decorated by the designer, Alvin Lustig, as a discrete framework for the Japanese sculptures of the Heian or Kamakura periods, for the Tang horse, for the precious Noh masks, for the shaman of Vera Cruz – and for Chagall, Braque, Chi Pai Chi, Roerich and Orozco. So, on two occasions when the body needed to feel "at home," after the accident and for a few years before he died, we stayed in New York.

It was in the library surrounding our bed that Bill kept his favorite books. He loved to read and reread (sometimes aloud) the Heart Sutra. "In emptiness there is no form, no sensation, no perception." Often before sleeping he would take down a large red book by Sri Atmananda (whom we called irreverently "the Policeman"), open it at random and read to me the questions and answers. And there was also Meister Eckhardt, whom Dr. Suzuki admired. Another link with Dr. Suzuki was the Eastern Buddhist, the magazine that he had created at Otani University before the war. We subscribed to it in Paris and New York and had collected all the numbers from its first issue in 1938. Bill thought this magazine was essential. He often found new commentaries in it by our friend Norman Waddell, and the writings of his favorite Japanese Zen Masters of the past—Dogen, Hakuin, Bankei. And of course the whole Gurdjieffian library was there, too. Other times, it was poetry that took his attention, in anthologies of Chinese, French or English poets. His favorite French writer from his youth was Montaigne.

Han Lady

Chester

Bill had bought Chester in the forties because of its proximity to Mendham where Ouspensky was installed at Franklin Farms. He said that he bought it without even seeing the house, seduced by the waterfall, the pond and the woods. We had family reunions there. He loved to play the "pater familias" on occasions like Thanksgiving, Christmas and the New Year, when his two daughters, their husbands and children would come for a few days. After skating on the pond, we liked to gather around the fireplace in the living room, or take a sauna after Bill and his grandson, Max had patiently prepared the fire.

There were two little buildings in the woods at Chester: the meditation house and the studio where we painted—he in oils and I in pastels. That was the studio where we would organize the pictures for exhibitions in the nineties, after making and gilding the frames.

Before breakfast each morning and at sunset each evening, Bill would go to the "quiet house" by the lake to meditate. On weekends when about twenty "pupils" would come to Chester, the first meditation took place very early, and everybody arrived punctually, even after driving for two hours or more at dawn.

In Chester, Bill had a complete workshop, with a collection of beautiful Japanese saws, some of them hand-made. He loved wood, cutting up tree trunks into fire wood, or working on this living material. We would often work together, stacking the large quantity of wood we needed for fire places, kitchen and sauna.

Bill collected all kinds of tools in the garage and the basement. He would always walk around the thirty acres with a secateur, trimming branches where needed, showing that the hand of the master had passed by. The Chester property was very poetic. William Segal – Painter, *the first of the three films Ken Burns made about Bill, shows this so well. The little pond with its Japanese lantern, the meditation house, the painting studio in the middle of the woods . . . and Bill in his Panama hat, drawing amidst this calm and tranquil natural setting.*

Fire Island

Fire Island offered a very different atmosphere. In the thirties, a few artists, writers and painters like Bill had discovered this island was ideal for writing a book, doing some creative work or just resting unobserved. At that time, there was no electricity and no telephone lines. An hour's travel from New York, it is an island without any cars. So you get around on foot or by bicycle. Here Bill conceived and constructed more than one magazine. He painted this picturesque place, with the dunes, the pines, the sand and water.

In all these comings and goings (we would travel without luggage), the only complication was Suki. Suki was a green parrot from the Amazon given to him by his two, then adolescent daughters. To transport Suki, Bill had built a little wooden box pierced with holes to let in the air, and as we drove from one place to the other by car, Suki would methodically chew the wood, which Bill would methodically repair. So Suki's box became a showcase of bits and pieces.

Oil, 1938

Paris

As soon as we arrived in Paris, Bill would go directly to the room in the back of the apartment and would begin to paint. "With this light, anyone can be a painter," he often said. The windows opened to the north, with a view of the National Assembly and, in the distance, Sacré Coeur.

My apartment, 8 Place du Palais Bourbon happened to be across the street from where P.D. Ouspensky used to live, the Hotel de Bourgogne et Montana.

It was in Paris that Bill developed his taste for lithography. In 1980, he began working at the famous Mourlot atelier. But when he felt that it had become too commercial, he shifted to the more modest workshop of Jacques de Champfleury where he worked directly on the stone. He would take the subway nearly every day to the workshop in the remote 19th arrondissement. He loved to tell about his lunches in popular Arab restaurants where, for only twenty francs, he got a complete meal with wine and coffee. When Bill became too frail to make the journey, Jacques brought the heavy stones to him in our apartment, and that is how the "Conference of the Pots" was made.

les flics sur la place

Sometimes we would go exploring in a district we did not know. Bill would stop to admire the cast iron balustrades, each different, unique. He would always choose a spot where there was a market. "Our" market on rue Clerc was within walking distance across the Invalides esplanade. Bill had become friendly with the fishmonger there who, each time, would explain to him how to cut and open the sea urchins. Bill often met with Madame de Salzmann. They would have dinner together and seemed happy to speak quietly of the past, present and future of the "Work," and of the questions closest to their hearts. His Gurdjieffian friends became mine, and all my friends had the most affectionate admiration for him and the depth of his insights. They loved his elegance and originality, his monocle and his eye patch.

8 Place du Palais Bourbon

I remember our last three weeks in Paris at the end of March, 2000. The year before he had strongly expressed the desire to make "a last visit" to Paris and to travel on the "old" Concorde, the only way for him to cross the Atlantic. Since he had proposed to accompany me to Paris, I had accepted a job to create stage sets for the production of L'Avare at the Comedie Francaise. Bill seemed delighted by my new profession. So when February 2000 came, we took the Concorde. We were happy to leave for Paris one more time. But on our arrival, we did not drive as usual to the little bistro on the rue St. Dominique to begin our day with foaming coffee and a tartine. Instead, Bill took at once to bed.

One month passed. Bill was becoming more and more fragile. Breathing was difficult and he had no more energy. He was always cold and stayed in his armchair by the fireplace in the living room where wood was burning all day. He said to me, "Let's go back to New York. I don't want to die in Paris." So we took the Concorde back, but I had to return to Paris to finish my work. Our friend Patricia, like a real daughter, offered to stay with Bill, who often said to her, "When is Marielle coming back? I'll have to stick around a little more." Those three weeks of absence were torture for me. I flew back to New York while the paint was still wet on the sets. I found him with no more life energy, yet so present.

Meeting Peter Brook in Paris

Life in Four Places:

Place du Palais
Bourbon, Paris VII

Chester, N.J.

150 East 69th St.,
New York City

Abigail,
Maxmilian,
Jonathan,
WCS, MBS,
Raphaël,
Margaret and
Elizabeth
in Seaview,
Fire Island

Bill
paterfamilias

VI the painter

Every painter is different in what he likes to paint. Some a poor orphan child, some a mother and child with a dog, some the horrors of war. The self-portrait is really a search for the 'who am I.'   –WCS

An American Painter

It is truly hard to describe my astonishment when I discovered a large number of Bill's paintings in the attic of the house in Chester during one of my first visits. Most of them were devoted to Bill's three favorite subjects: landscapes, still lives, and portraits. I took them all down to the kitchen and washed them off with soap and water. The paintings revealed a simple, direct vision, without complicated effects or technical bravura. I came to the United States in 1948 to study American painting, and here I was, twenty years later, seeing my husband's work, a perfect example of what had interested me in the first place.

When I asked Bill a few questions, he answered laconically, "I've always painted." It was an intimate secret part of his life while he was a businessman. A comment from Cecil Lubbell, his former editor a propos of Bill's 1999 exhibition at Tibet House, says it well:

"The self-portraits take me back some fifty years. I was editing Men's Reporter Magazine (1945-49). Our photographer, an ebullient young Irishman, wanted to take some indoor shots with natural light and Bill offered the use of a studio he still rented on 14th Street. It was a surprise to me and even more so when we got to the studio because there I found, stacked against the wall several canvases with self-portraits of Bill in various Picasso-like poses. I was a bit embarrassed about this because I felt I was penetrating a secret world unknown to me, and far removed from the commercialism of men's fashions. So it impressed me."

As in so many domains, Bill was self-made, he was a self-made painter, and did not belong to any stylistic "ism" of his time. He did not seem to be a member of any special school, although he was for a short time trained in the famous classes of Nikolaides.

When he began to be serious about exhibiting his paintings, in the 1930's, Bill provoked enthusiastic reviews, both in group exhibitions and in his one-man show at the Lenox Gallery in 1937. But after he met Ouspensky and began his spiritual search, he was less interested in exhibiting his work, although he continued to paint incessantly. The painter

William Segal the painter looks at the
outside world and leads us into
William Segal the man.
He seems to paint what he sees, but
looking out he is looking in and happily
he invites us to do the same.
The play of his forms,
the harmony of his colours
his spaces and his silences
all take us
to a secret meditative core.
This core has no name, we are touched
because it belongs to us all
and yet its expression is unique
and arises
in one unique creator.
Art is soul.

Peter Brook

*Orozco became one of his good friends, and they traveled to
Florence together, studying frescoes.*

*His artistic production continued into the 1940's, but with
less recognition, as critical attention became increasingly
focused on Abstract Expressionism.*

*In the early 50's and into the 60's he spent considerable time
in Japan, immersed in the Eastern Arts. His long friendship
with the Buddhist scholar, D.T. Suzuki, led to close contacts
with Zen art. Unquestionably these influences, filtered through
a purely American temperament, deeply affected his later
work. Space, time and the revelation of a reality rooted in the
void are problems he finds well suited to the medium of expression within his search.*

*After 1980, having recovered from his accident and having
shed his responsibilities at the magazines, Bill began to paint
again very seriously. For a dozen years he accumulated drawings, portraits, and landscapes. Bill came to enjoy lithography
and made a great number of prints. So in 1991, at the suggestion of his friend, the designer, Bill Bonnell, he had an exhibition in Stamford, Connecticut called "50 years of American
Painting." In this exhibition of more than 80 works there was
a large self-portrait he had worked on for a very long time. It
was a particularly strong painting, showing him in a favorite old
sweater, and I really wanted to keep it for myself. So the gallery
marked in NFS—not for sale. But one day the gallery called;
someone wanted to buy it. I found out who the someone was: the
filmmaker Ken Burns. Since we admired his work immensely,
the painting left and a dear friendship arrived.*

*A number of exhibitions followed in his later years, in Tokyo,
Paris, Jerusalem and New York. But in 1995 his energy began
to fail, and so he turned from painting to drawing. We would
assemble the elements of a still-life together; bread, eggs, a fruit
or two, a salt shaker, a knife and a number of goblets and
glasses. The light of Paris shining through these glasses gave a
name to an exhibition in Paris in 1997—"Transparencies."
His last exhibition, "Sixty years of Self Portraits," at Tibet
House in New York, in 1999, was called "In Search of Self,"
the preoccupation of a lifetime.*

163

Luminosity

In painting one is brought to see in a different way. Ordinarily, we're asleep to the world around us. Being forced to look and then to render with paint and paper, compels one to see both inward and outward, to learn a little more about oneself as well as learning about the nature of things.

The painter's part is to reveal the potentiality of the everyday objects around him. The seemingly familiar things, events, surroundings, take on a different quality when the painter looks at them, and this different quality can be conveyed through the painter to the spectator.

Cezanne is able to show us there's an awful lot here . . . right here . . . in everything around us . . . not ruling anything out. Shown the potentiality in this small piece of fruit, the intelligent person may be able to grasp the fact that there is a whole world around us of beauty, of interest, of complexity. I'm being fed just by looking, and yet it is here before me every day. I don't touch it, I don't see it, I don't see its color. In other words, it's a jumping off point for a greater openness to the wonderful world we live in.

Luminosity is a reflection of a higher world, which sometimes enters your world and my world through a face, through an apple, through a painting. It is always here, this luminosity, but it's so densely hidden. Luminosity is all around us in everything. The painter, with a certain quality in himself, is able to evoke this on canvas.

One day in the studio. I had been painting for three or four hours, just painting. Suddenly it was as if the brush was painting by itself—I stepped back in surprise—I stopped, and there was a beautiful piece of painting within a bad large painting. I suddenly said to myself there is something here that goes beyond applying paint on a canvas.

It is indicated to me that through continuing to paint, persisting, there will come a moment where there is an opening which can teach what I cannot speak about. As if one suddenly knows something—maybe not much—but you know something that you didn't know before. And at that moment I said, well, I have to keep going.

```
perhaps
   purr haps
            the greatest artist
   of
   our
   century
            will prove to be

      WILLIAM SEGAL

   who painted a
      transformative
               PEAR
   but
if we feel honest
   with us
      may we
            DISCOVER
         all our moments are
               TRANSFORMATIVE?

   Segal is immortal
         but
         are
         you?

Our answer is hoestly
            surely
```

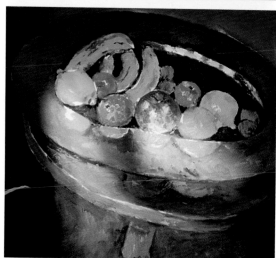

There is a risk in self-portraiture. We see our own reflections countless times a day—in mirrors and windows everywhere we go. And we are curious, pleased, critical, vain. But we rarely have the courage William Segal has, the courage of self-portraiture, to ask with each fleeting glimpse of oneself: Who am I?

—Ken Burns

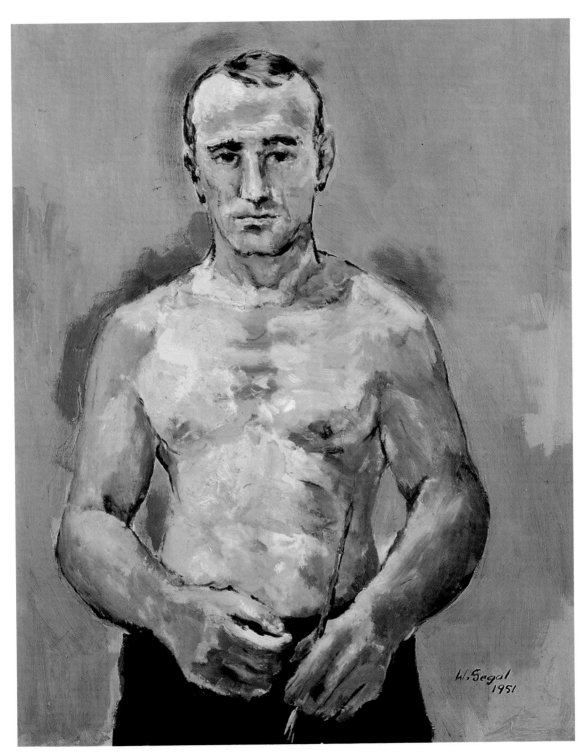

1938

Sixty Years of Self-Portraits

A Conversation with Mark Magill

MM: In your writings, you make a statement about the importance of being still a few moments before beginning.

WCS: It is my belief that every one of us is a vessel that contains a very great energy which goes unattended. Right now as we sit here, there is something in us that is waiting to be called. And if we attend to it, if we acknowledge it, we will then be in touch with a force that can illuminate. It can transform and shape each one of us and can help to change the world. When one is still and one listens, then one begins to be in touch with this mysterious element which is within each one of us.

MM: After that moment of stillness, one goes into action . . . ?

WCS: Yes, even in action, the stillness is always here. The point is that we don't listen to it. It doesn't make any difference what the action is. In the background, in the interior of oneself, there is always this vibration, this energy which can change things ultimately, and transform them in an upward direction. So that's always here, in action or when one is still. Of course it's easier if one is still, quiet, when there's silence, when one is not taken by the stress and by the impact of our modern lives. But unfortunately we live in New York City in 1999, where human beings have a tougher time in contacting and relating to this still element. It's possible that it was simpler in other times and circumstances, but it's up to us to function where we are.

MM: I have the impression in looking at your work that there seems to be a search for this "moment."

WCS: Would you agree with me that most of the time we're distracted? If the outside doesn't distract us, then

1935

1995

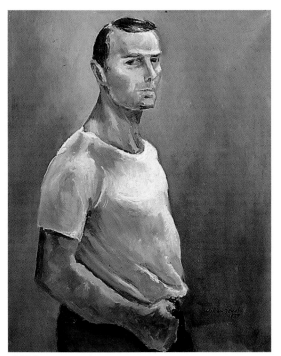

1938

the average human being is distracted by the constant associations, the so-called thinking which goes on. So when I speak of this moment, this wholehearted attention to now brings a concentration of energy which is quite different from our ordinary state of dispersion. Right now I'm speaking to you. At the same time I know I've got a house full of cares to worry about and things that will take my attention, but now I'm speaking to you. I'm sitting here. My feet are on the floor. Being here is the most important element in truly functioning as a human being. Otherwise, we're all over the map. That's why we say some people have no weight. They're not present. With other people, one feels their presence and that is because they are related to this great energy which is in each one of us. So being here is the beginning.

MM: Do you find the practice of painting is a particular help in this "being here?"

WCS: Yes, whether it's painting, or carpentry, or doing a physical job, the point is to do whatever one does with

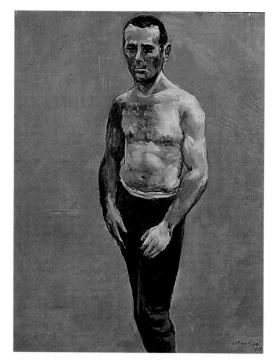 

"One is the outward flesh form, the other, a man in red pants and a blue shirt, a mysterious creature wandering around in limbo, in strange colors, looking for himself."

—WCS

one's whole attention, and painting forces one to bring a special degree of attention to what one is doing. You have to be there. The practice of attending wholeheartedly to the moment is most important. I think there's a biblical saying, isn't there, "To do whatever you do with all your heart and all your might?" It refers to being present and attentive. No things are large and small. Everything is important, whether I'm buttoning my shirt or drinking my coffee in the morning. A certain degree of attentiveness is very important.

MM: In the case of Rembrandt's self portraits, for example, is there something transmitted about the kind of attention you're speaking about?

WCS: I think Rembrandt is one of the great examples of a gifted man, who eventually came to realize that concentration, attention, and presence brought an element to his painting that went beyond the technical virtuosity. He was always a great painter and probably he could paint without thinking too much. But I think that the more he looked, the more he began to see beneath the

1930

1990

surface. So when he did his self-portraits, one feels that he was able to penetrate through the exterior surface, to very great mysteries and knowledge. And by applying himself totally, he was able to bring this into paint and canvas, into a form to which we then respond.

MM: There is a mystery in that, isn't there?

WCS: I suppose that's the mystery that makes life more interesting. There's something going on beyond the visible, but I'm not always in touch with it. When the crowds go through the Metropolitan and view the paintings, one has to admit that it's rather a surface examination. We take a quick glance. "Oh that's beautiful, that's wonderful." But not enough has been seen. Not enough has penetrated. Our perceptions are not very strong, generally. And we suffer from that, because all of this is a kind of food. It would be interesting to examine how we are when we walk in a museum. How we look at a painting. How we look at an object. There's infinitely more than—what did Shakespeare say—"More than meets the eye?"

MM: That brings us to the subject of your self-portraits. Is there a special significance in using your own form as a subject?

WCS: The human face is very interesting, at least for me. Every face, ugly or fair, provides a model of complexity. As I look at you, the eyes are marvelous, the shape of the nose and the texture of the hair are intriguing. All of these elements coming together are worthy of trying to probe and see what they represent. There is something else there. And this something else is the greatness of each human being. The form will dissolve over time. We die and get chucked on the manure heap. But there is something that animates us. We all know the difference between a dead body and a live body, between a man who's present and a man who's sleeping. On another level, my face is always there. I can always turn to a mirror. Instead of setting up a still life, I look in the mirror.

172

"Looking into the mirror, it is it looking into you looking into it into you into."
—Peyton Houston

Fire Island, 1992

Marine Gallery, Tokyo, 1993

173

MM: In looking at your work just now, there are sixty years' worth of self-portraits gathered together. Do you see a thread leading from one to another? Do you see something that's changed?

WCS: Yes, I think there's a subtle change, as you put it. There has been a change from a young man with an ordinary psyche to a man who's in search. It's difficult to speak about oneself that way, but I think I see a change towards a seriousness of search that was not present sixty years ago. In a sense, I was always looking. But there's a maturity that the years bring which makes the difference.

MM: You've said that in painting, one grows richer by leaving things out. What is it you're leaving out?

WCS: That's a whole subject in itself. Because, like music, it's the spaces in between the sounds that make the music. By leaving things out, you enable the viewer to fill in with his own thought, his own imagination. On another level, don't you think we tend to fill our lives with the nonessential? One of the Gurdjieff teachings, for example, is: one ought not to do what is not necessary. These non-essential items tend to clog up the mind and prevent one from being in touch with a quite different reality. We become preoccupied with the trivialities most. Leaving an empty space adds another dimension. So you leave space. And this empty space leaves room for the relationship between oneself and this other vibration to take place. Otherwise, it's impossible to come to anything real.

MM: Some years ago you suffered a serious automobile accident. I understand that some Tibetans rejoice after a misfortune. For them, it's paying the debt of bad karma by suffering misfortune now. For some of us, that way of thinking might look like an upside-down view: relishing misfortune and suffering.

WCS: This idea of an "upside-down view" is very interesting. After all, there's no good or bad fortune. Everything is in flux, everything changes. There's always, in every event, the other end of the stick. So be careful of your good fortune.

MM: What I suggest is that in the practice of art, struggle is an essential ingredient. In that sense, it could be seen as an upside-down view, to welcome the difficulties.

WCS: One has to accept giving up something for the sake of something else. In other words, I give up my laziness, I give up my desire for comfort because I know that out of nothing comes nothing. After all, I am lazy by nature. I don't want to paint. I don't want to study. I don't want to go against myself. But by going against oneself one develops capacities that one doesn't ordinarily know exist.

MM: It seems that facing a blank canvas is a way of posing yourself with a challenge.

WCS: It's true. When one is in front of a blank canvas, where do you begin? It requires an effort of pulling oneself together, of calling upon all of one's faculties. It's not so easy to start a canvas and to go on with it. There is a saying: "Burden me, that I may grow strong." At the same time, this God element is in each one of us. But there are many paths. It's possible one could just go blindly through life and not engage in a struggle. "Don't burden yourself with it. Just take everything as it comes." And one can still come in touch with this. One school advocates struggle, hardships, and austerities and another says, "That's alright, I'm a child of God. Let what comes, come."

MM: Are there many painters who hold that view?

WCS: Most painters are just painters. They have an artistic temperament or they have a talent or they want fame. They want to be able to create. That's another category. I think that on the different levels of mankind, the painter is relatively high. But he is still just below the level of the seeker. I think I was able at one time to say to myself, "Oh, my God, I don't have to paint." I had come to understand that I was painting because I was looking for something. I was searching. And then one day I woke up and I said, "I don't have to paint. I could just be." And at the same time I was drawn back to painting, probably by egoistic wishes. After all, you want to be somebody in the world. Of course it's a great occupation, too, isn't it? I've had many businesses and conducted many affairs and I find that painting does occupy the entire man. So in that way it intrigues me. But, after all, even Rembrandt's works are going to disappear. I have no illusions about myself. At the same time, yes, I have. I want my family, my descendants to say, "That old man was not too bad a painter."

MM: You've said that salvation consists of living without being dominated by one's ego. We were just speaking about the ego entering into your work. So it's an aim, to find that kind of salvation. How does painting serve that aim?

WCS: It calls on the use of all your faculties. Otherwise, I'm wasting what should not be wasted. The potentiality for the transformation of the human being is continually present. But unless one exercises as many of his faculties as he can, these possibilities are not really fulfilled. So as a human being, I would like to function at my peak, without the intrusion of egoism. In other words, I wouldn't be seduced by thoughts of glory, money, or fame. So in painting, if one is rigorous enough to apply oneself—to be non-judgmental from one point of view and very judgmental from another—in that sense, I think the practice of painting is ego-reducing.

MM: You speak of being non-judgmental in the act of painting and seriously, severely judgmental. You have to continually make decisions. Something is making these decisions. How do you know you're on the right track, or can you know that?

WCS: I would say that one might know it by the realization that one is not totally scattered in one's thinking. That one has not lost the concentration, the attention. That one continues to be aware in the moment, instead of saying, "I want a drink now. I'm going to call up my friend and we're going to have lunch." The challenge of painting calls you back. And there's the end result. Somehow you know when you're doing a good job. In painting, I think the results are visible. After all, I'm not insensitive to the finished work or to work in progress. I say, "This is all scattered. I'm just not here. I'm not doing well."

MM: How do you know when you're finished?

WCS: It's hard to know because one is tempted. Still, one knows when one is proceeding mechanically. One has an inkling. When one realizes, "Oh, I'm just painting. I'm not being attentive enough. I'm not here enough," then you better stop. Otherwise you're going to spoil it. Most painters, most of us, spoil our work by doing too much. So it's a good question, when to stop. But look. (Pause). I've stopped talking. And I realize that I've talked too much. We have a self-critical element within us that can make this judgment, but it's probably not used well enough. It's a loaded question.

MM: That's why it's at the end.

WCS: Yes, how to stop. Maybe one could find the right moment, if one simply pauses and takes a few breaths. Then one may come in touch with stillness. And in the silence, one is better able to make a judgment, a judgment in the true sense. But we're not sufficiently in touch with that.

Arizona, 1950

178

Friendship and Painting with Harry Herring

I first met Harry Herring in a business way. I became an editor around 1926 upon graduation from New York University. One day a large man came into our office and introduced himself to me as a purveyor of engravings for our company, which was planning a magazine called Plastics. Plastics was a new substance which was just being introduced into the States. Harry and I became friends. Besides being editor, I was in charge of ordering art work and engravings. I soon learned that he was a well-known painter and active in the contemporary circles. One day he suggested that perhaps we would sketch together and employ a model to do live poses. Friendship with him developed to the point where we started to share a studio and began to go on sketching and painting trips together. He was a typical self-made man of his time, head of a large successful photo and engraving business. Still, his chief interest was in painting and particularly in the American school of art. I recall that most recognition was given to French painters and that he resented strongly the fact of the neglect of the Americans.

He could never bring himself to move into the modern movement in art, and so kept what he called the seeding attitude in relation to art. He said: "You see. You can put it down and find something in anything." He was a very quick painter. He could sketch a landscape, a face or a group scene very quickly and most of his emphasis was on drawing rather than color. Naturally, our mutual interest brought us together in a wider sense.

He exhibited regularly at the Frank & Rahn Gallery, which was probably the most important art gallery of the period. But he was never successful in the selling way, although his work was very highly regarded among the painters. The lady who ran the Museum of Modern Art also showed great appreciation of his work. Mrs. Whitney, who started the Whitney Museum, considered him one of the best American artists, but his kind of work never became popular. At that time all the

Harry Herring by WCS

American artists were superseded by modernists like Motherwell. I saw him a day before he died and he had become blind. There he was, this big bulk of a man, alone. It was rather sad.

The trips we made together were very interesting because we got into a car and would drive straight down to Georgia or Virginia. I still have some paintings and sketches in the savannah surrounding Georgia. We were both extremely quick painters and it was nothing doing six oil canvases besides some sketches. We were both physically very strong and could move and work from dawn to dusk. We could keep painting all day. So we took these trips periodically in our car with our stuff stowed away in our baggage.

An Exchange with Painter, Paul Reynard

PR: Why do you paint? What is the impulse for a painter? Why not sit . . . Why not grow carrots?

WCS: Very good question. Why does one paint?

PR: What is the impulse? When you began painting, sixty or seventy years ago, why? Why did you choose painting, why not violin, why no trumpet? Why painting?

WCS: I think that the complexities involved in painting are much greater, and offer more possibilities than say, growing carrots. You grow carrots, and you have to dig the earth, then you wait, and you wait; but in painting each moment is threatening and challenging. The challenge is so great that it evokes different energies. When one saws wood, that is very fine, but it has its limitations as far as stirring up new vistas of energy or of possibilities in one . . . it is as if we never use totally, we never exercise the potential of our combined faculties. Painting challenges to such an extent that new combinations of energies are aroused.

PR: Composing music, too . . .

WCS: Music of course, is a supreme art.

PR: Do you write? Do you write poems?

WCS: I am not a writer. I write poems, but writing is not the natural "elan" for me. Speaking of "the natural thing," the use of the hand is important! A painter has to work physically with materials, brushes, canvas. All that physical effort moves into the creative effort. It keeps you very much alive—it is very much a three-centered activity. Even physically you have to keep pushing yourself.

PR: How about background?

WCS: The background is very important. Everybody looks at the object. But the object is really not separated from the background itself, it does not exist in a vacuum. When you know it practically, you can know it philosophically, and even esoterically. Our energies are not isolated. If you ask someone, "How about the emotional center?" one cannot put and hold the emotional center in one's hand like an egg. It is involved, connected with the mental, the physical and psychic centers.

PR: Do you feel that you have to be very quick when you are observing a still life? Is there something that is quickening? Is a question of quickness, or . . . there is a movement there, saying that I have to be aware; is it threatening, because I cannot stay vivid?

WCS: Yes. That's why I keep emphasizing the factor of attention. Generally, relationships are only glimpsed. But if you stay with it, you begin to see more subtle rela-

Louis Nizer

Tony Provost

tionships, how this has an effect on that, how this color affects that color. So, the whole world makes for an enlarged, rich new world of impressions. Then you enter into it, or it enters into you. Lacking impressions, we go through life half starved. Cezanne could get so interested, and see so much in the apple, that he could be fed all morning by impressions coming to him from an apple. Energy, coming from attention, makes for a rich or a poor life, results in transformations, and in developing the great scale. We are speaking of small things, but big elements are also involved; the principles are the same. One little grain here . . . like Rene Daumal's book, "Mount Analogue," where the bee takes the wasp, and makes one small movement that results eventually in an avalanche, or an earthquake.

PR: Is it better not to be a theorist of painting?

WCS: Theorists and critics are not painters.

PR: I work with painting for which there are really no words.

WCS: "One picture is worth a thousand words." You may see something in a sketch, which is very revealing and would have to write a book to describe the psychology of a rogue that is revealed in Gericault's portrait of a man. The subject's whole character, his life history, are in that one picture. When Toulouse-Lautrec draws a chorus girl, a night club singer, you grasp the whole ambiance, the morality, and the life of Paris at that special time. So there is a mysterious conveyance that does not need a lot of words.

PR:: Do you agree with Kandinsky, who says that blues are colors for spirituality?

WCS: It may be Kandinsky's particular bias. I am always happy with cerulean blue and Naples yellow—separately and together, as a combination. Some colors seem to have more spiritual value than others. Maybe this is Kandinsky's finding for himself, but I'm not sure it's a set principle for everybody. I find I gravitate to hues of blue and to the complementary combinations. One is on solid ground with combinations of blues and yellows, the reds and the greens, blacks and whites, violets and oranges.

PR: Are there any special writings you would recommend for young artists?

WCS: I have been greatly helped by reading Delacroix. His diary clarified many things that were not obvious to me. In going over some old paintings I saw too much preoccupation with details. Delacroix points out it that is necessary to paint with thought. Thought helps to say what you want to say, and results in freedom from small details which often cloud the painter's larger vision, freedom that comes from a pure attention. One more naturally moves towards a wider view, towards a broader way of painting—without losing freshness and the nuances, which bring joy to the viewer. Delacroix also elaborates on the struggle between emphasizing the drawing and letting go with color—of letting one or another predominate. I was stuck for a number of years, drawing, neglecting to see the potential of color.

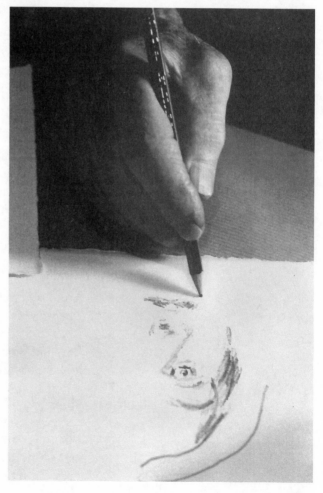

Toward the Essence

The smallest object–seen–represents order and beauty

Both the advantage and the privilege of an artist is that he is forced to look. To see. People rarely see the beauty and the greatness around them. They live their lives in half sleep.

The factor of attention is never given enough weight in painting or in other aspects of human activity. With attention the artist is able to go deeper into the potentialities of the subject. Attention, well developed, equips him with the capacity to be open to what would ordinarily escape him. The technique of painting, complicated and difficult as it is, can be learned by man. But the average attention span is too short, and attention is easily diverted; the ability to "see" is rarely deep enough.

With sustained attention, one grasps relationships which usually are overlooked. So how to nurture an attention which penetrates into the heart of things? It's an interesting subject, to speculate that with attention. Whole new worlds reveal themselves. The Chinese and Japanese artists have understood for a long time the importance of being "still," of gathering their energies for a few moments before beginning.

Instead of a headlong rush, which is fine for a while, one has to step back. This stepping back is difficult, especially when one is on a roll. In painting, as in other pursuits, when all is going well one wants to keep going... that's fine, but sometimes a pause, stop, stepping back and looking brings the unexpected.

Moments of stillness align one's forces. When man's energies are together in balance, more is possible than when they are random, dis-equilibrated. Heart and feeling are needed as well as the intellect. Concentration, attention is the key in any endeavor, whether building a brick wall, working with a computer program or painting a picture.

The artist is fortunate in that he can find and give meaning to the humblest encounter. No subject is too small, too insignificant, to receive his attention and care. In the sense that behind appearances there is another reality, the artist may be said to resemble God. To be true he must approach the subject with "pure seeing." Always there is seduction of the mind-gravitation toward the unknown. With inside-seeing we awaken to the beauty and the potentiality of ordinary objects.

The emergence of light from an area on the canvas always intrigues. The painter cannot evoke this by technique and virtuosity alone. It does not work that way. It is the total absorption of the artist in the work that enables true luminosity to appear.

There is no nonsense about a still life, a solitary object. You can keep looking at it. It gives you a chance to really be there to find out how deep you can go.

As one works, order appears out of the chaos. It may be difficult at the beginning. As the process itself takes over, there is such an absorption, you forget your mother, your father, your dinner, everything. Here one has to be careful. There are certain moments when it is better to stop, to be mindful of the space on the canvas; not to fill in everything. In leaving some things unsaid, a work of art reaches toward the essence. It was the mystery of the visible and the hidden that drew me to lithography, a medium where economy of means, what is not stated, is of keen importance.

Ritual of lithograph signing,
Atelier J. de Champfleury

Lithographs, Paris 1997
Exhibition, "Transparences"

Working on the book, *Transparences,* printed in
lithograph at Atelier de Champfleury

VII on the Gurdjieff work

WCS, Peter Brook and Michel de Salzmann, Paris, 1993

Moving stones, Silver Lake, 2000

On the Gurdjieff Work

A Conversation with Peter Brook and Michel de Salzmann

WCS: It's interesting to go back to one's first recollections of a meeting with a man of the stature of Mr. Gurdjieff. I recall his entry into the P.D. Ouspensky estate in Franklin Farms. There were a number of people waiting for him. One felt the movement of the atmosphere around him as he entered the magnificent hall. What struck me immediately was the presence. Then he did something that was very revealing to me. He looked around the table and he saw the lords and the ladies, the people who were preeminent in Ouspensky's work at that time. And he said, "Who is in the kitchen? Bring out the people who are in the kitchen doing the work." It struck me immediately as a demonstration of the democratic attitude of this really unusual character. He could size up people, a situation, the truth of the moment. One had to respect that. I was trained as a journalist and I had the experience of meeting a number of spiritual characters around the world. But there was something very different about Mr. Gurdjieff. Absolutely no pretense. He was an authentic spiritual master. This was the feeling that I received on first contact. Am I speaking too much?

PB: On the contrary. It begins to make a picture that comes to life. Please go on.

WCS: I didn't get to know him as well as some of the other people, but I recall one incident that was rather amusing. I was doing movements in Carnegie Hall and, by chance, I was in the first row. I wasn't fit to be in the first row. I didn't know the movements. I saw Mr. Gurdjieff. He had a look that said, "Who is this man doing them all wrong and botching up this beautiful class?" He advanced towards me and as he got close he raised his arm as if to strike me. At that moment, I had the revelation, this is really an extraordinary moment of both playing and seriousness. I had a moment of absolute freedom from fear, from considering what he thought or what other people thought. And he, of course, demonstrated a very interesting sense of humor. He looked at me and smiled, as if to say, "Oh, you're hopeless, but nevertheless, nevertheless . . ."

At this stage of my life, I see that Mr. Gurdjieff's long-range vision was absolutely correct. He foresaw that the Western people were not quite ready to understand Self. He was preparing the way, through emphasis on exercises and practices, of remembering, of being aware of oneself. At first, one felt this in a vague sense. But as we went on I could see better what was taking place. I firmly believe that his way, which is the Fourth Way, will take hold in one sense or another in the West and will accomplish, perhaps, what he had hoped.

MS: You, yourself, have been involved in this work for half a century.

WCS: Yes.

MS: You've also helped hundreds of people to find their way in their search within themselves and also into a "real world," as it is said. And in your heart, what would you say is there? In other words, what is the specificity of the teaching for you?

WCS: It's to be related to the highest in one's self. If one is capable of maintaining this relationship with this vibration, this other force, it will change the world as it changes the individual. It isn't as if I will become a better painter or you will become a better physician in one great leap. But there will be another element brought into relationships and to one's life.

PB: Can I pose Michel's same question slightly differently? In what way is this a progressive teaching? Somebody arrives completely from the outside, having been touched remotely, deeply but without knowing why, and then that person enters into a process. As in every religion and teaching what in this work are the specific steps?

WCS: I would put it on a very down-to-earth basis. Here is a cup of tea. It serves its function. But with attention, with awareness, which is the bedrock of practice of every esoteric teaching, the range and the depth of impressions increases to a remarkable extent. I think that I was prepared to appreciate this specificity of the Gurdjieff teaching because of my early training as a journalist and a painter. I knew that if one could just look, a whole world comes into being. And from that point of view, the inner world of one's self begins to play a part in one's everyday activities.

MS: Yes, and to come back again to the same question, that of self-remembering. You placed it at a very high level. The Supreme Identity, so to say. And at the same time, to reach that, there is a start, a self-remembering that is already meaningful in the beginning. And one sees this sort of progression that Peter speaks of. The steps are of self-remembering, so to speak.

WCS: I believe that self-remembering should be looked at from the view of different levels. There is a simple awareness. I know I am sitting in a chair. You and I are speaking. And then there is a widening, an inclusion of the body, of the atmosphere, of the surroundings, so that the impressions are richer. There is another dimension which begins to be added to our relationship. This relationship with this inner, (I call it the Savior), the center of God, the center of a higher element. When that is present, there is an opening towards a richer, freer relationship with one's self, with others, with the world. I think we move towards our destiny as human beings when this relationship exists. Otherwise, I am dependent on a brain, the feelings, the body, the different minds and centers in my organism. But when this relationship is made, when one is able to include the other, another dimension enters.

MS: Is it specific also, that approach in all the conditions of life?

WCS: Here I'm rather a pessimist, a pessimistic optimist. I think it's very difficult, taking into consideration

Michel de Salzmann   WCS

the stresses of human existence in the 1990's. The difficulties which the average person faces make it almost impossible to develop the sensitivity and awareness necessary to relate to this principle that we've been speaking about. That's why I think there is still a great popularity of feeling for Zen Buddhism. There was a specific training. But that training involved going into a monastery and spending a period of time developing one's capacity to be here. Gurdjieff's system takes into account that we are limited in our possibility for practice. Listening to this glass clink is a practice. The conversation, the body itself, the moment to moment awareness, however one is able to follow that. And so over a period or time, one indirectly comes to have this capacity, comes to have this acute awareness. I speak of it as if it is something you put in your hand. I don't mean it that way.

PB: When I first heard of the work, they had a method called "the method." First it was called "the method," then "the system," then "the teaching," then "the Work." It's clear there is a very delicate balance between "methods" and the step by step progression towards the state when it is possible quite simply to hold a cup of tea and look at another person. How do you see the Work as a teaching?

WCS: From my present point of view, I see the immensity of the Work and its implications for the world. But the actual nuts and bolts practice is to be as present as one can at each moment. It's Gurdjieff's "remembering one's self" and Zen Buddhism's "every minute Zen." They're not very far apart. But there is no guarantee that there will be a leap to the other relationship. Gurdjieff's teaching has one wonderful advantage in that it includes different sides of the human psyche. For some people, movements, for example, are very necessary. For some people it's necessary to approach and to see the implications of the teaching through the mind. There are many different approaches in the Gurdjieff way, but always there's a movement towards greater awareness. Any

Dr. D.T. Suzuki

serious follower of the Gurdjieff teaching will arrive at that.

MS: Yes, Chogyam Trungpa puts it as meditation in action, of which you are an example.

WCS: I don't know that I am an example. But you're absolutely right. This moment is a meditation. Just as, on the other hand, one can be sitting in a monastery in a formal position and there will be no meditation. There will be the movement of the mind, not only movement of the feelings, but the mind itself moving, moving. This is not meditation. Even though I sit for six hours.

MS: Your deep knowledge of Zen Buddhism, your friendship with many roshis and your frequent stays in Japan, all this goes well with the Gurdjieff teaching?

WCS: Yes. When Mr. Gurdjieff died, I was a friend of the Buddhist scholar D.T. Suzuki. He gave me letters of introduction to six different Zen monasteries and said "If you are really interested, here are the letters. Go there and stay as long as you want." I felt the Zen people had something that we didn't have. On the other hand, as I became more and more friendly with the different Zen masters, I saw the great respect they had for the Gurdjieff teaching and for Madame de Salzmann's way of conducting Mr. Gurdjieff's work after he died. Almost unanimously, the Zen masters I knew were especially interested in the Gurdjieff movements, if they knew about them. Suzuki and I went to several movement films and classes together. He said, "You know, Zen and Gurdjieff are very close." Speaking subjectively, being an American, I'm negative on robes and ceremonies. I respond very much to Gurdjieff's approach of, "I'm just a doctor or I'm just a carpenter, I'm just a bus conductor. Meanwhile, I'm doing my meditation in life while I conduct this bus." So, that part of it appealed to me, the indirect practice that is taking place if one really practices the Gurdjieff work. We're at the point, though, Michel, Peter, where it's really up to us to see what comes out of this deeper relationship with the inner world.

Jeanne de Salzmann

Michel de Salzmann   WCS

MS: I wonder, is there a rigor, and what is it, the rigor in the Work of Gurdjieff?

WCS: The rigor of the Work is to be continuously listening, listening to another vibration while going about one's everyday activities. That's the real rigor for me. It's not movements, and it's not groups and it's not the writing of pamphlets or books. It's the capacity to encompass the inner world, which we have very little knowledge of, and the everyday world. The world of form and the formless.

MS: How does this capacity, so essential, develop?

WCS: I think the Gurdjieff method can serve your wishes. There's a balance that's as effective as we can have in the ambiance of our present civilization. I believe the average citizen of the western world is in a bad spot. He's harassed by many things. All he can do is to take in so much at a time, by going to groups, going against oneself, trying as one knows in one's own way to remember one's self, to be aware, to practice sensation, and so on. All these ways may seem slow and indirect, but I think they will eventually lead one to the brink where you leap over the precipice and you make your own discovery. Eventually the teacher is in one's self.

PB: What was your experience coming back from the Zen monasteries to the practices of the Work? What did you find in making the link between a very pure, nameless experience and of these different practices?

WCS: I must confess that I was a great proponent of meditation, which I felt was lacking in the Gurdjieff Work in the 1940's. I was in Japan in 1952. I had my own experience after three or four months in the headquarters of the Soto Zen Monastery. I came out and said, "My God, I've been in the Gurdjieff work for seven or eight years, and here after three months, I made a leap." I felt that this practice of formal sitting of Zazen was lacking in the Gurdjieff Work at the time. Then Madame de Salzmann did institute it. She probably had that practice going in its own way, but I felt it needed a more formal adherence. We needed more "sittings." Trying to speak from the moment, as we do in our practice and in the groups, leads one to the same place. It's not very clear but one doesn't obviously say, "Oh yes, I'm in touch with something."

WCS   Peggy Flinsch

PB: No, we don't. If, on the one hand, in Zen, there is this particularity you speak of, working with others in a group has something that doesn't exist in Zen and which has its own path. Do you feel that a group has something very specific?

WCS: I think it does. There are groups and discussions, but the form of the Gurdjieff Work is quite specific and quite indigenous to the Gurdjieff teaching. This is where the group leaders also have a possibility of learning from the people in front of them. Probably the real group leader learns more from the groups than they learn from him or her. But this idea of being on the spot, with your back against the wall, can make an opening that cannot be made by a simple exchange of ideas. In a group, there is the possibility of moments in the exchange where something is really learned beyond the ideas. The Gurdjieff ideas are all available. One can read about them. But the personal encounter between the student and the teacher is very important. This does take place in groups. What's not understood in groups, I feel, is that the prime necessity for the guide, the group leader, is to make the people work, while he's working. In other words, giving the answers is not really very important. But the answer should carry with it an impulse to work, or even force to work.

Dr. William Welch   WCS

MS: Yes, that is the real point.

WCS: The hearer has to work on himself. Otherwise, why exchange information? Madame de Salzmann was a great adherent of that. I remember almost the last thing she told me. She said, "Make them work." She also said, "Don't give them answers." She didn't believe in giving answers. "Make them work." That impressed me. It's the guts of the system. Because you're making yourself work. I can't make you work unless I work.

MS: Working together has a special effect, doesn't it? Working together brings the mysterious element of help.

WCS: I think that is a very important point. And we are at that point now. Unless we are together, we limit ourselves. Coming together, we see the lacks, we see the potentiality, we see the level we are not at, and we are all helped by this exchange among ourselves, by this coming together. I think it would be a pity if we separated and each one set up his own little fiefdom. That's why I would like to see greater circulation among ourselves.

MS: Maybe this is one of the specificities of the Gurdjieff Work. The demand to work together.

WCS: Yes. This could be. Mme. de Salzmann was able to do that because she had the authority. But now we have to find the authority among ourselves, to bring about relationships that are right to maintain the truth of the Work, the spiritual. Otherwise, the odds are against us.

PB: Do you think there is a work, on the vastest level, to be accomplished everywhere? It is easy to say that in the heart of every esoteric teaching there is exactly the same truth, but isn't there a difference between what Zen suggests that there is a quality without movement that is at its finest in monastic conditions—and Indian thought, which says that the highest of energies is always needed to activate the movements of the world? The sense that one can only fulfill man's destiny by responding to a dynamic cosmic need seems to be at the root of Gurdjieff's "All and Everything."

WCS: There is, perhaps, a flaw in an approach to work that is making this entirely an inner process and hoping that it will be manifest in the outer. But I do think that we're at a point where the inner should manifest itself in the creation of the outer form. One has a dynamic inner life. And it circulates among a limited group of people. But the outer creation could be touched by the inner. In other words, we should be coming to the point where the outer works will speak too. I mean the film that's being made, the book that's being written, the plays that you do. Otherwise, the call is not strong enough, unless one sees the visible manifestations of the invisible.

PB: It is manifestation for the sake of the world.

MS: Painting for you is a good support for that. For living. I mean inner support.

WCS: Painting is the devil, Michel, for me. In other words, when I paint, I'm always seduced by the form and by the practice of the craft itself. If I trusted God enough, I would really be a good painter. But I don't. In painting, one has the possibility to join the two worlds. And there is a result. I think Rembrandt was able to come to that. Rembrandt was able to be in touch with the other world while manipulating the brush and the oil paint. And so you have a miracle. It's the intensification of the inner work. In other words, one puts oneself on the spot. I can say, "I am in touch with my inner world, I am remembering myself or I am praying." But then I have to write what I think I understand and when I write it, there's an extra demand. I intensify my effort.

MS: Yes, it's for the sake of circulation of the good through us and through the world.

WCS: Otherwise we live in ourselves. It's painful when I see the behavior of people, including my own. I say, how can she set a table like that? How could he produce a book of this nature? It reflects something of the inner. But we seem to have a special role that we could play, if we're able to play it. Whether we will it or not, I don't know. I'm speaking of the Gurdjieff teaching.

MS: In his last years, there were a lot of highly talented people around him. It took them decades to understand better what he brought to them and also to be able to transmit something alive. This was a group of very good people, talented beings, innerly developed. Now most of these people have disappeared. Only a few are left. What would be your hope for the continuation of the teaching?

WCS: It's difficult for us to judge from our present vantage point. You see, you and I were looking at these people when you were twenty-two and I was thirty-two. They were already pretty high up in their respective professions and endeavors, but maybe right now there are people in the Gurdjieff Work who are producing creditable work. In any case, there isn't any question in my mind that there is a heightening of the sensitivity and the spirituality of these people as a whole. One sees a refinement taking place in people that was not present twenty or thirty years ago.

MS: That's right.

WCS: After all, who are we? We are rather ordinary people and yet you see that this girl or this man is now somebody.

MS: This is the miracle. From that very high call, the Work has developed. That means the majority of people have become much more developed.

WCS: And this is an indication of Madame de Salzmann's efforts. After all, we were really a pretty rough crowd of people.

MS: But, in a way, today they undergo less strenuous discipline and efforts than the older ones.

WCS: Yes, that's an interesting question. What's more strenuous or less strenuous? Or what is more effective or less effective? Is it the amount of time? Is it the going against oneself? It's really the intelligence of the effort that's in question.

MS: Absolutely.

WCS: Not so much the donkey work for the body or the stupid going against oneself. On the other hand, the basic principles of the Gurdjieff teaching should never be lost sight of, as for example, the necessity for physical work for men. It's very important to establish a sexual orientation of a right nature, to establish a soundness of a physical life, going against oneself. It may be that we are erring on the side of a failure to provide a more rigorous orientation at a certain point in the Work. In other words, a period of two or three or four weeks of real rigor, away from the world, away from the chaos.

MS: Yes.

WCS: It might be helpful. Because you and I are a different breed in a way. I remember we really could work around the clock physically and perform things which we hardly see any young man capable of doing. I don't know much about women, but I think the women are all right. They're always ahead of the men. The big question is, what do you do when there is nothing you can do? Which is equivalent to mind and body dropped off in meditation. Nothing you can do. There is no support of ideas. No support of practice.

MS: This is probably where the breakthrough appears.

WCS: It could be. But people get nervous when they hear that.

MS: This meeting may also call another taste, the super-effort, as it is called. It is not understood very easily, the meaning of super-effort.

WCS: Don't you think that Mr. Gurdjieff sowed the seed for understanding that by his idea of stop? When he said "Stop," there was nothing you could do. The implication was, "Don't try to do anything. Stop!" That for me was a foretaste of mind and body dropped off.

MS: Yes, immediately, one has an impression.

WCS: Of the silence. The real silence. I think that we lose the point when, as you said, we should go into this self-remembering. The self is probably the unborn

Buddha mind, never born, never dying, always is. We deprive ourselves of this relationship. Yet all this is very temporary. Anyway, we all need about three hundred more years.

MS: Your first contact with the Work, the Work ideas, was Ouspensky, wasn't it?

WCS: Yes. I very greatly admired Mr. Ouspensky. He came into my life at a time when I was looking for something without knowing I was looking for something. Of course, he was bringing Mr. Gurdjieff's ideas, but I liked the way he thought, the rigor, the coherent way he had of expressing himself, the wide esoteric knowledge he had. And he was a regular fellow in many ways. We had a very good relationship.

PB: Where was that? In Franklin Farms?

WCS: Yes. He thought I was a real journalist and so I think I was one of the first Americans he liked. He would talk to me as if I were a writer. I think I was one of the very few Americans that would go drinking with him at night at Longchamps at 59th Street. I could see many things about him. And yet I don't think he got it. He had everything. He had ideas. He had theories.

MS: A brilliant mind, evidently.

WCS: A brilliant mind. He had experience, but I think the relationship with the other world was not his chief concern. His chief concern was the development of an idea.

MS: Understanding?

WCS: The understanding of Mr. Gurdjieff's ideas. But he was a wonderful man. I don't know why people don't give him his due.

PB: Did you see him in this very strange, last period of his life?

WCS: No. But I can tell you about one encounter the day before he sailed. I was plastering a wall in Mendham. He came by, I'll never forget this, and he said, "What are you doing?" I said, " I am just fixing up the wall." I was a fresco painter, so I knew how to plaster. He said "Why don't you come to England with me, we have wonderful fishing?" I said to myself what do you mean "fishing?" I pondered that. I still don't know what he meant. I'm not a fisherman, you know. He seemed a little bit strange at that time. And that was the last time I saw him. There's something sad about Ouspensky. At that time we never heard about Mr. Gurdjieff. It is a very strange thing. Mrs. Howarth was the first one to speak about him. She said, "What would you do if you met a teacher who was greater than Mr. Ouspensky?" I said I'd have to meet him first before I'd know what to do. But she added, "You're going to be up against somebody now. Not Mr. Ouspensky. You'll meet a real teacher." I remember that conversation. I didn't believe her.

MS: It's about forty years ago that you met Mr. Gurdjieff. You were engaged in worldly action. What did you learn from this meeting?

WCS: This is a question which is frequently asked. In all candor, I would say that the most important thing I learned from Mr. Gurdjieff was in the Turkish bath.

MS: How?

WCS: He had a custom of going regularly to the Turkish bath accompanied by several of the older men. To this day I remember the picture of Mr. Gurdjieff, walking in the atmosphere of steam. It was from his back, from the way he walked that I learned something. Which, perhaps, is not possible to explain. Something of the true nature of an enlightened person if you wish. But not in those words at all. Some time ago in Japan I paid a visit to the widow of an old Roshi friend of mine, Kobori. The new Roshi was there and I asked him the question, more or less the way you asked me, "What did you learn from your master? How do you know that you will be capable of carrying on the teaching of Roshi Kobori?" He turned his back and said, "When I'm able to impart the teaching with my back." I was struck by the curious similarity of Mr. Gurdjieff's back imparting teaching in the West and this Roshi saying the same thing.

MS: What he said is wonderful.

WCS: It's a strange coincidence. But, of course studying the ideas of Gurdjieff and verifying them through one's own experience is essential. It always struck me that there was something quite different about Mr. Gurdjieff. After all, he didn't say anything. But to me, directly, he said a great deal through his Work. So, it must be that he had a relationship with his inner world that was so strong, that it emanated, reached and touched others.

MS: I believe that there are two aspects which the Gurdjieff teaching clearly distinguishes, conscience and objective consciousness. Intellectual consciousness is a very high level of consciousness. We can see that Gurdjieff evoked both. Is one higher than the other? This is a question, but evidently the two overlap. In Gurdjieff's teaching there's this notion of conscience. It means this intelligence of the feeling that arises some-times and makes us feel what is, and also "conscious-ness," which is something quite different, in a way. One should say "supraconsciousness," in fact, because it's not ordinary consciousness. And so, the teaching stresses these two aspects. Don't you think he was an awakener of both?

WCS: Yes, but perhaps you might say that there are three expressions: conscience, consciousness and super-consciousness. Unfortunately, there is a slight misun-derstanding of the meaning of the word conscience between the French interpretation and the English interpretation. But Gurdjieff's teaching of the idea of conscience being awakened is all important. Because unless conscience is touched, there is no stirring of the emotions, no opening towards conscience in the English sense of the word. Consciousness is, as we take the word, the awareness, the being here. But I can be aware of being here and not be aware of the superconscious element, as you termed it, in myself. At this moment I can be aware that I'm here but without being aware of this, of consciousness in the ultimate sense. For me, this is the part of the Gurdjieff teaching that enables us to have a relationship with Consciousness, which, as I said before, changes everything. This is the famous remembering of Self. This is the remembering of "Who am I?" Not just the creature sitting here. I think that it is the role of conscience to awaken one to this question of "Who am I?" In my ordinary unawakened state, it's always "I, me, mine." Suddenly a teacher comes and there's an opening towards the Self, the I, quite different from the small self who wants something for himself. On the path to awakening in a true sense, there is always the necessity to have this acute attention to awaken to oneself, to remember oneself. In this moment, I may or may not be remembering myself, you may or may not be remembering yourself.

MS: Yes, because, "Who am I?" is not a formal question.

WCS: It's an unanswerable question.

MS: It's a movement, isn't it? A movement of entering.

WCS: Towards an opening.

MS: Yes.

WCS: Towards the mystery of why we're here. And who are we really? All teachings inevitably come to this question. Which is the only approach to the solution of problems of both the individual and of mankind. Do you agree with that?

MS: But again, one realizes how long it takes one man to engage himself and give himself totally to this question, to the Way.

WCS: Yes.

MS: And we see fewer and fewer people ready to engage their lives into that questioning. I wonder how the teaching can touch enough people. In the present circumstances, it's really a question. Maybe not for everybody to be lived and experienced in that way, but something must be given, shared by other people and one wonders how.

WCS: Does it relate back to the question of conscience which we spoke about?

MS: Absolutely.

WCS: The masses of people are beginning to realize the horrible, the catastrophic situation which we've come to, because of the lack of a universal teaching. We've come to a century where there is the recognition that there may be no way out, except through conscience being touched and opened.

MS: I think it's very important what you say now.

WCS: Yes, I wish I could make it clearer. But there is a process going on. And perhaps in this age of communication, the message is being absorbed by more people than we realize. The true necessity is for those people who have been in contact with ideas or religious systems, whatever they are, to be truer and to go deeper into this question of who we are and what are we here for. I think this is important. It is the recognition that life is not only "I, me, mine."

MS: Yes. Of course, the Gurdjieff teaching is like all the other teachings, extended in some way. Near Gurdjieff there was just a small nucleus of people coming from America, from England, from France as well as some who followed him from Russia. And it was Madame de Salzmann who brought along many people, many people in France during the war, and all the talented people that were around her. Centers were created in most of the cities. Mainly first in New York, London, Paris. And from there, an expansion. So there was something that was done to have an action in the world.

WCS: It's been rightly said that Mr. Gurdjieff sowed the seeds, bringing the teaching to the West. And the seeds have been sowed. But it was Madame de Salzmann who watered the fledgling plants over the past few decades. From my travels I see the results. The fruits are beginning to appear. There are more people with more understanding. More of Mr. Gurdjieff's ideas have been subtly infiltrated. So I can see that the work that Mr. Gurdjieff initiated and Madame de Salzmann cultivated is well rooted. We probably will not see the widespread effects for a few more decades, but they are bound to appear.

MS: When Gurdjieff came to America, there was a very great interest. Many intellectuals came around his table.

WCS: Frank Lloyd Wright was one.

MS: All the people came. It must have been an interesting situation. Were you there to see that?

WCS: I was there, of course, after World War II, when he appeared in New York. It was really an event. He came in that bitter cold winter of 1948. There was something stirring which we all felt. I'm not sure we were ready, but at least the intelligentsia was very eager to know more about the teaching and, of course, people were fascinated by his charismatic personality. The way his teaching was carried on was quite unique. Lunches and dinners at the Hotel Wellington until two or three in the morning. People clustered around the table, asking questions, being subjected to his sometimes rather biting remarks. It was a ferment which one felt, very strongly.

MS: And it remained discreet. Nobody knew about it. There were no novelists who would write about it.

WCS: That's true. It was quite discreet. It was all happening within the sixty square meters around him, one might say. The impact was very clear. There were articles appearing in the New York press as far back as 1949. But the stir which he created was within limited circles. I don't think the impact was felt outside of this limited number of people.

MS: Yes, at that time the influence was very much underground.

WCS: Very much.

MS: Many trends in philosophy or psychology were influenced by the ideas.

WCS: Yes.

MS: Without reference to the source.

WCS: It's extraordinary. In the span of thirty or forty years there's been a burgeoning of the ideas, an infiltration of the ideas, in the universities and the philosophy courses, the psychological teachings of other people. And other people feed off his ideas without knowing it. Why are you interested in that aspect? Are you doubtful that the teaching will not continue to have its influence? It's reasonable to doubt.

MS: I think it all depends on the quality of people. There were at that time really a great number of people of great quality, and little by little they disappeared. So one must have confidence, trust in the new generations.

WCS: One should trust not so much in the new generations as in the truth of the basic ideas in the teaching. The development of the capacity for attention is very important.

MS: But it can be altered so quickly.

WCS: How do you mean that? Altered?

MS: An idea can be presented and be diluted and become very ordinary.

WCS: Yes. But always there will be, as there should be, a nucleus of people who will adhere to the main principles and the main idea, the main aim of the teaching. What is a man? We only see the surface, the shell. All the potential of the human is overlooked. But Mr. Gurdjieff never overlooked this. Incidentally, when I say he never overlooked the human, people to this day underestimate the suffering that he underwent to bring this teaching to others. I remember him near the end of his life walking out of a room after dinner. I think you were there. And he practically fell down. He took hold of my arm and he

Work at Armonk, N.Y. in the 1960s

said, "I'm tired." Of course he was tired. He was giving of himself, night after night, to literally scores of people. You were there. You know that. I felt this, too, about Madame de Salzmann.

MS: You say that what makes a man is the capacity of his questioning.

WCS: Yes.

MS: You said, "Who am I?"

WCS: Yes.

MS: And one could see that when someone had a question, maybe not as deep as that one but in the direction of that one, this is when Gurdjieff was really glad. Hearing that in a person. In other ways, giving attention to the person and letting him feel that this was right, that he was touching something true.

WCS: Yes. Of course, when one thinks of it, isn't it the most absorbing question that a human being can have? To know what we're here for. One can choose to be a banker or teacher, but the question for a human being that's the most absorbing one is, who are we? It's a fascinating study. Why do we go into art, music and poetry? Why are we interested in all the things that make up the human existence? Love, eating, drinking. Inevitably they are all directed, I believe, towards the question of who we really are.

MS: What I want to say is that what makes a man is his ability to question himself. And when someone at Mr. Gurdjieff's table really did that in front of him, you would see him smile with a special kindness emanating from him, because an authentic question had arisen. Really, that is what sustained him the most.

WCS: You know, a propos of that, I remember when I was a young man reading about Napoleon and Goethe. Napolean said something very interesting when Goethe walked into the room, "Ah, voila un homme!" He didn't say he was a strong man, a beautiful man, a rich man or a talented man. He said "Voila un homme." This is the specificity again; when you see someone like Gurdjieff, Madame de Salzmann or one of those roshis, or some of our contemporaries, you say, "This is a man!" This is a quality that accompanies consciousness, this is the fruit that I hope will arise from Gurdjieff's original appearance in the West.

MS: Mr. Segal, thank you for what you have brought us.

"Sittings" and the Gurdjieff Work

A Conversation with James George

JG: I was going to ask you, to start with, about your role in helping the introduction of sitting as part of our Work. This needs clarification for posterity, and you might like to comment on the sameness and the difference between traditional sittings say, in a Zen-do, and a Gurdjieff sitting.

WCS: My view is that Madame de Salzmann, in an effort to help the sittings become truly effective, took a most indirect approach. In first introducing the sittings to Group One, for example, she refrained from announcing that any formal or structured sittings were taking place. We gathered together and she would speak of the importance of correct physical posture. She would make comments as to the necessity of relaxing and so on. At no time, as I recall, were sittings as meditation labeled as such.

So this was a very indirect introduction to the idea of sittings. After a while, we realized that sittings needed some guidance, especially for people unfamiliar with them. She provided the guidance in the form of taking our mind off the "self-conscious sitting." In other words, we find today that in many people who take up meditation, there's a self-conscious element that interferes with a true sitting.

I think sittings often take into account the outer forms, but a true sitting is very difficult. A true sitting, in my estimation, would be a choiceless seeing of what is taking place as moment by moment passes. A true sitting means an unflagging attention coming from a still place in oneself. There's no judgement, no grasping. There's no wishing even, just sitting. I don't suppose that in this respect our sittings differ very much from what advanced Zen meditations would be.

WCS and James George

Perhaps the difference between Zen and Gurdjieff sittings lies in our recognition that people need guidance. The mind needs a little help in being tethered. One speaks of being able to stop thoughts and control the mind, but this is very difficult. So while the attention is on the words of the guide—the man or the woman guiding the sitting—there is less tendency for the mind to run off.

I would say that, apart from the guided element, there's not much difference in sittings of the Gurdjieff people and the Zen people.

JG: I think there is a difference in the fact that in a

Gurdjieff sitting, the guidance continues through the period of sitting. In other traditions, I think it's mostly instruction given before you begin sitting, and then you sit quietly. Wouldn't you find that corresponds to your experience?

WCS: The one difference is that during the sitting sessions, there are intervals when punctuation is used, such as the whack on the back or a sharp clack of noise-makers used by Zen practitioners.

JG: I think that is very similar, yes.

WCS: With us, the one guiding the sitting has an inspiration that something is needed at a particular moment, to wake people up or to bring them to another level of realization. This really is the great art in giving a sitting which very few people have understood or mastered. There's a moment, after a period of about ten minutes of silence, when one says just the right word which reverberates around the room and touches all people.

One can't say what this word is, but there are moments when one is inspired to say the right word, and this is a feature of the Gurdjieff sittings. I doubt whether we'll be able to keep this up but I think there are a few people able now to punctuate a sitting with an appropriate comment coming at the right time.

JG: You doubt that we'll be able to keep that up?

WCS: It depends on people. I think that the sittings are an on-going development in the sense that there will be changes, maybe of a subtle nature, but there will be changes or adaptations to the particular circumstances and time. Each sitting is different and it's almost impossible to give any formula for a sitting. This is probably the danger to our sittings today—that we attempt to make them fit into a pattern.

JG: I think that is a danger because then it ties us to a past memory instead of to a present sensitivity.

WCS: There are imitations. Someone thinks it went well and something happened at one moment at one particular time, and then you attempt to repeat. Nothing is repeatable. So if the creative aspect of sitting is taken into account, it means that there is an on-going basic sitting with slight, but very important, comments or additions or whatever it is that can be brought into the sitting. It can be anything. It can be a cough, it can be a clapping of hands, a bell ringing—but those things are artificial.

JG: Michel (de Salzmann) has sometimes used Tibetan cymbals.

WCS: That may be good, too. But it brings up associations. I believe each sitting is unique in itself.

JG: It's as if we were trying to be empty to receive what is always there. In that sense, I still have the hope that it may be possible to pass on some of that sensitivity without it automatically going down to the level of imitation.

WCS: There's a spontaneity you can't recall or bring back. You can't memorize—or repeat. You can't imitate. Spontaneity comes from a true relationship with the silence. We come back to the basic instruction, which is to be aware of the body, the breathing and the stillness. If one is true enough, from the stillness, from the emptiness itself, comes the "mot juste" that could be brought into the sitting; the feeling of something that can only spring from the stillness.

JG: There is so much life and possibility in that stillness. We never are in touch with it enough. I don't instinctively share the pessimism of some people who feel that, inevitably, there is going to be a deterioration in the way we work and the way we understand.

WCS: In any case, what's behind the silence is always there. We may lose contact with it but it will inevitably arise to touch people again and again, because there is no time-space connected with it.

JG: It's omnipresent?

WCS: That's right. The "omnipresent okidanokh" is probably the silence.

JG: That's a very interesting thought.

JG: Tao, as has been said, is untranslatable even in Chinese. It's beyond our understanding. But I think the parallel is there.

WCS: Probably the same thing. We give it different names. In every religion and every discipline we're speaking about the same things but we have no words to describe no-thing, emptiness, instead of stillness. It's the emptiness that gives birth to everything, creates everything.

It is strange—I'm sure everyone has had the experience, "Why do some moments come alive?" Madame de Salzmann and Mr. Gurdjieff were able to make all moments more alive. They were always in touch with their essence. And we are touched as soon as someone else is touched. But everything is reachable. Probably there is no iota of materiality that can't be touched.

JG: In your life experience of the Work, from 1941 to 1996, you've seen a change—a change in the way people work. I wonder if you would like to reminisce about the way the Work has changed and shifted, how it has grown. . . and why.

WCS: It sounds very arrogant to say this, but I believe that it was post-Gurdjieff and post-Ouspensky that the true sense of the Work began to be understood. We all were attracted by the idea of esotericism. The search was true in everybody and was effectively nurtured and guided by the early founders. But the feeling for the presence (or the possibility of presence) in each individual, and the importance of presence, was not emphasized enough in the earlier period.

In other words, what I'm saying is that, while Madame de Salzmann knew all along what many of us were vaguely feeling, at the same time, much of our understanding was based on seeing our own lack of understanding. We really didn't know what remembering was. Each one took his own definition of self-remembering as finality. We had been hovering about the idea and we did have vague feelings about what it was, what it is to remember ourselves. That accounts for the compassionate view that I'm sure our teachers had for us. Obviously we couldn't understand what was beyond us. And suddenly we reached a point where a handful began to catch on. We're still hovering around the idea but I think it's much more conveyable from one to another. The practice is more extensive than ever before in the history of the Gurdjieff Work. So from 1941 to 1996, there were people who were catching on. I don't think there were so many in the early days.

JG: You mentioned, critically, the self-conscious sitting. In fact, the whole mode of working with an ego involvement towards a spiritual goal has been—certainly for me—a big handicap, an obstacle. You mentioned how important it has become to understand presence, but I think we're also coming to a quite fresh understanding of ego as well, and the obstacle that ego can be to presence. How would you comment on that? Is there a need for ego? Or is it just an automatic resistance that we have to struggle with on the road to presence?

WCS: I'm not certain I understand the whole question of ego and egoism. I think it is a necessity for life and I think none of us are immune to it. From the moment we are born, it is cultivated in us and it has its place. I've ceased to think about ego. It's there. It doesn't matter. It doesn't make any difference. It's not "It," anyway. So I don't bother myself about it. But that doesn't mean it isn't a big obstacle, and a big help at the same time to getting what you want. Ego drives one, of course, and on the other hand, the ego blocks one. I'm so close to the end of my life, I'm just concerned with the necessary.

JG: Coming in the same direction myself, I also feel the weakening of that ego. I'm not grasping in the way that I used to.

WCS: One sees the evanescence, the ephemeral aspects of life. What is the difference whether you are the President of the United States or if you are the richest man on earth or even the most learned man? That's not it. So why waste our time on putting out our chests, receiving medals or writing a book? It's all right. Such manifestations please our friends and our relatives.

JG: It was very subtle for Gurdjieff to present the object of search as "I." Nothing could appeal more to the highly individualistic culture in which we've all been brought up and live. But how to understand that "I" as individuality and not as ego, and live accordingly?

WCS: You know there was a man, who on his deathbed said something like, "Nothing matters." I don't think that's the whole answer, but there's a lot of truth in that, in relation to the question of ego. Nothing matters and everything matters at the same time. But there are questions of life and death—what do the great religious people say about life after death?

JG: In some traditions, they speak of the drop going into the ocean. In fact, Gurdjieff also uses the two rivers going into the nether regions or into the great ocean of destiny. Something that I don't understand and wish to understand—are higher-being bodies, or whatever it is that is formed in us when we work, is that individuality? Is that the real I? How can the drop that goes into the ocean retain its individuality? Or is there something individual that really can persist?

WCS: I wouldn't know. I can't say.

JG: Our focus in the Gurdjieff teaching is not concerned with that very much, but...

WCS: I think what's implied there is that individuals might develop memory. And this memory may be part of a vibration that survives the death of the physical body.

JG: So that next time around, one doesn't make all the same mistakes?

WCS And one contributes to an upward movement of the universe. I don't think time exists there.

JG: What is the most inspiring thing about the establishment of the Gurdjieff Work in America?

WCS: What do you think?

JG: Whenever in history, humanity has faced a particular period of crisis, there have been teachings given to get us over the danger zone. And for me the excitement of this Work has always been the sense that we were riding in the Ark, and privileged to have found it; that we needed a special teaching for this special time and this is it. The traditional teachings are very good, but in order to understand them we need a new language today. And this Work is a new language—indeed, a new teaching for our time.

WCS: Now we see the crisis has deepened.

JG: And we see the inadequacy of many of the so-called "New Age teachings." As they've been popularized, they've been frittered away and trivialized compared to what is needed, which is a much more serious, rigorous, disciplined spirituality. And I think our Work does offer that.

WCS: Do we face that fact that we have not made much of an impact—certainly as far as numbers are concerned?

JG: We must. And I would hope that we are on the verge of an expansion of influence, not a contraction. I think that's possible now, if we wish it, but it seems ironic to me that so few people even wish it, think of it as possible.

WCS: Don't you think that the teachings themselves have filtered into the life of the people? There are more people willing to accept ideas. Ideas which seemed very radical, are now more or less accepted, such as the idea that man cannot do, the idea of the individual being composed of many "I's."

A sane method of living could be one of the great contributions. And what is a sane method of living? To cultivate a high level of awareness of the self, of one's presence. All teachings emphasize that without seeing, without being aware, without having an attention and awakedness, we miss the mark. There is wrong doing, wrong living, as opposed to right doing, right living and thinking.

Then there is the idea of "being"—the idea that a man's

being is more important than his possessions has taken hold to a degree. Most of us don't value the man who says, "I'm the richest man in the community. I'm the most powerful man," But on the other hand, we don't seem to come to a true evaluation of being.

JG: The awareness you're speaking about breeds a kind of sensitivity in our culture. Sensitivity to being. Mostly people are sensitive to how much money you have in your pocket, and how many cars you have and all that. But not to being.

WCS: There were periods in history when we lived more poetically, more artistically, more becomingly generally. On the other hand, it's not a terribly bad period, is it?

JG: Not yet. I feel it's going to get worse.

WCS: We certainly don't value money-grubbing. We don't value power-possessing, domination of others by so-called strong people. We do respond to charitable impulses, to appeals for help in the community and so on. What we should do is arrange on one side all the plusses in our society, and on the other all the minuses, the negatives.

JG: Have a look at them. And should we do the same thing in looking at our Work? There are our weaknesses as well as our strengths.

WCS: What would you say are the weaknesses? The weaknesses would be those of any society, wouldn't you say? Laziness, lethargy of a kind, not being involved enough, not working hard enough. But everything depends on the state of awakeness.

JG: I think one of the weaknesses is not really being aware of each other enough in a compassionate way. There hasn't been much mutual help. I could give examples . . .

WCS: There may have been wrong interpretation of non-identification. At Franklin Farms, it was shocking—the lack of feeling for each other. I thought it came from an English coldness—from the idea that you don't identify, that the body doesn't count, the physical, outer exterior condition of a man or woman, whether one is poor, rich or famous, is not important. It leads to a great deal of questioning . . .

What you're saying is that there's a certain lack of warmth among our people, for each other. On the other hand, I don't know, but it seems there's a good feeling among many of the young people, isn't there?

JG: I think so. Working on oneself is all very well but working with others can be just as important.

WCS: Yes. When one works with others, one is working with oneself. I agree with you, we are pretty cold towards each other. I can say that it would be wonderful to meet a man who was free of ego. Once in a while we come close to meeting such people, but they are few and far between.

JG: Huston Smith was being interviewed on PBS by Bill Moyers, who was talking about various traditional examples of the perfect being, the Jivanmukhta in the Indian tradition. And Huston Smith said, "I don't really believe any of that. There is imperfection built into our greatest saints, because we're human. And in this body, that's the way it is. There's no such thing as a perfect human being." What do you think about that from our point of view? I mean, there were imperfections in Gurdjieff himself. He made it very obvious so that we wouldn't worship him, as the Indians worship a Jivanmukhta.

WCS: I would put it that there are moments of being in the Work. There are moments of being a perfect being, but we do revert to other moments when we are not. As Mme. de Salzmann said, "We must serve with a more objective feeling, and at the same time serve with one's subjective feeling. Both are necessary."

VIII in search of silence

I remember seeing my first Noh play in Kyoto almost fifty years ago. I was absolutely struck by the initial appearance of the main player. It was the moment when he was crossing the bridge that separates the back of the stage from the stage itself. His was not the walk of an ordinary man. It sprang, instead, from an inner relatedness. It gave rise to a tension that became almost unbearable, bringing the audience to a high degree of attention. All its concentration was focused on the deliberate movement of the slightly bent, robe-clad figure.

His voice, too, in the few words he spoke, carried a weight. This slowly moving figure produced a vibration that seemed to speak to each one in the audience. One could not escape the fact of being present to something different from our ordinary existence, a change in the conditions that were a result of the being of the player. Time was surely being examined in front of our eyes. One felt that something new was about to unfold. One passed a threshold in oneself from one part to another, to a different level of being.

It was a transformation. It was as if he was in between a world he had left and an entirely new world. In that moment he embodied a kind of stillness that is difficult to achieve in our everyday lives.

—WCS

Prayer and Silence

Prayer is here and now. Prayer is always concerned with the silence, the stillness.

Prayer is the expression of a human need. Prayer enables people to express their desire, at different levels, from supplication, wishing for something tangible, to a wish for nothing material, where the impulse is for the highest. Perhaps it is still asking, but what the highest prayer wishes for is unity with God, communion, supreme identity.

Prayer has to do with transformation. Transformation can only take place with a great effort, a commitment of time and knowledge. One transforms oneself from a captive of the associations of everyday life toward the highest energy, the indefinable.

Perfect meditation could be termed perfect prayer. A person in a state of purity, in a state of prayer, would be a person in meditation. There are no associations, the mind and the body are stilled, open to a force which might be called God. This openness to Godliness may be where one arrives after a period of deepest prayer, and deepest meditation.

There is a knowledge and effectiveness in a person who's come to a balanced state. A realization that "You are I and I am." There is no discrimination, no for or against; there is an acceptance of the "Is-ness" of things. One still sees the difference between the sparrow and the human being, but the man in this higher state is able to harmonize every aspect of himself.

The best conditions for praying would be a quiet place to sit, a relaxed erectness of posture, an awareness of breathing. There should be a balance of the energies of the organism; the mind free of associations, the feelings quiet, not tense. A state of balance is essential. The highest state is a progression toward being present—which means a silence, inward and outward. One is not apart from the inner silence.

There is an Islamic tale about Moses going to God to ask how many times a day people should pray. "A hundred," God answered, and Moses went back to his people, who told him, "It is impossible—go back and ask again." Moses went back and forth until God finally reduced the number to five. And so it has been for the Muslims ever since. For others it may be quite different. But regularity is essential. A regular commitment to prayer. Ideally one should be praying at every moment. There is neither night nor day if one is in a proper relationship to this silence. This goes on whether one is sleeping or waking.

The ardent wish which can help one towards the ultimate comes more with youth. I think there is an openness in children. Bhagavan Maharishi tells of a child who was asked, "Did you say your prayers?" The child answered, "I don't have to say my prayers; I'm going to sleep now. Sleep is my prayer." The Maharishi agreed. Sleep is prayer. When you are in a sleep state, you don't have any wish, you don't have any ambition. Close to sleep you are close to prayer. You realize that when you are soundly sleeping you are well off. When one is truly asleep, one is out. One has no associations. The mind is tranquil. One is in the prayerful sleep state that the child spoke about. When one wakes up, immediately thought appears: "I want this." A desire comes in, an aggressive attitude, one is for or against something. The first thing upon waking should be stillness. The last moments before you go to sleep should bring you to a state of relaxation in body and mind, an emptying of thoughts and feelings. In waking up one should again be aware of one's state of consciousness. An awareness persists however sleepy one is.

What is advised by the Tibetan Buddhists for the moment of dying is a following of the light. And the following of the light requires an awareness, a being there. If there's fear, or a wish, one is not concentrated in one's attention towards the light; and it is this concentration and attention to the moment of dying that is important. One must be entirely present. No thinking about one's will, one's heirs, one's regrets.

Perhaps the ultimate prayer is the consciousness of light. When one says, "consciousness of light," this is objectification. In the ultimate prayer there is no object, no light, no thing as it says in the Heart Sutra. If we stop right now and are aware, without being aware of anything—that would be a very high state. As long as one objectifies, one hasn't reached the highest.

Prayer can diminish the amount of evil; though evil is also part of the scheme of things. It evidently has its place. We try to diminish it and to move towards a purity. Prayer has this effect. There is a Zen roshi's claim that "sleeping beside the waterfall, I stopped the war."

Gurdjieff said that by going into a church and by opening yourself, being aware, you can receive an energy which has been deposited by people in prayer. In a church, synagogue, temple, or any place where people have seriously launched prayer, the atmosphere is good. One benefits from the vibrations generated and deposited by others.

No matter what the religion, at the highest level prayer is related and emerges as a state of silence, inner silence, inner stillness. At a very high level one may believe that one is having a dialogue or directing a petition to God. Still, even this prayer is related to the tangible—something which one can objectify. This is emphasized in the Hannya Shingyo, the Buddhist Heart Sutra: "No prayer, no you, no me . . . no this, no that." It goes on until we come to "No thing. Nothing," where you can't put labels, you can't objectify. I think this view conceives of prayer as absolute emptiness, stillness.

The Search for Silence

Be still, and know that I am.

—Psalm 46, verse 10

When I was a young man and for the first time heard the sentence "A woman waits for me," I was struck by the inner silence which these words evoked. The essence of this silence continues to haunt me.

In these moments we come to feel each other's poetic existence. We feel part of something latent that calls, without effort on our part, towards a rally point where we come together in a wordless, relatively pure state. Not a word need be spoken. But there appears a link of understanding. It is as if the many minds and voices had melted into one—a universal convergence into a beneficent, soundless tone, uniting without intellection.

Sometimes this sound becomes hard to bear. We become nervous, even ashamed, to be quiet more than a moment. Still when it departs, it leaves us bathed of the pettiness of ordinary life. Rare though these moments may be, they leave an impression on both the individual and the group. How blessed we are when we receive them.

Our capacity to remain open is very much in question, because we are trained to accept the mechanical flow of attention all the time. Mind is kept busy, forever caught in swirling thoughts. Mind, however, is subject to training. It can be occupied in such a way that it becomes controlled. When one thinks with intention, one is not subject to the shifts and incessant breakages in thought. There is less distraction and the consequent veering away of the attention. With a quiet mind and body, a stability and groundedness appear.

The breath can be a great support. Awareness of the breath gives a foretaste of stillness.

In the listening, the silence itself becomes a material that is available for transformation. We are on the way to being more unified.

One can gain a sense of this harmony and stability by observing some of the silent figures of the Buddhas.

They convey a stillness that is not easily disturbed, unlike the grass, which quivers with each gust of wind.

This gravity comes from a harmony of mind, body, and feelings. For most of us, there is an imbalance between the different parts. One part is too overbearing, another part is not functioning as it should. Each shift in thought disturbs the pattern of inner silence. We are ruffled and carried away by each wind. But when there is a balance among mind, body, and feelings, there appears a solidity and a concentration which does not permit of the frittering away of energy.

In a sense, we are called to live between two worlds, in a region which might be referred to as the Middle Ground—between the objective and subjective worlds. There is, in the silence of the subjective inner world, the possibility of being in touch with "I am." It is possible to encompass all the richness of impressions that are offered by nature and at the same time remain in contact with one's subjective "I." The complete man has access to a world of subtle and nourishing impressions. He goes on with his everyday occupations, but remains in contact with the inner world.

Maintaining this two-fold contact is difficult. The incessant appeal of the objective world constantly calls us away. We are continually seduced, mechanically reacting to sounds, both inner and outer. But always present, beyond the subtle breakages—the heart pumping, the breath, blood circulation, thoughts and tensions—there is the "other."

Going to the Quiet House

Chester, at Sunset

Quiet House

MBS: Tell me what you felt at this moment, when you were in the quiet house?

WCS: I had finished a short meditation in the quiet house, and as I came out, I thought I would sweep the broadway surrounding this house. As I swept in the afternoon sun, it was simply a moment of pure joy. At the same time, it was tinged with the recollection of the memory of even greater joys, if that were possible. The moment was still with beauty, perhaps because of the winter sun, and reflections on the small lake. In any case, I felt purer spirit going through me, and I was happy when I finished the sweeping to walk across the field and to see you, part of the landscape, part of the view. Can you hear the stillness?

MBS: Yes.

WCS: Can you hear the sound of the inner? The sound when there is no sound?

When we turn to anything other than God
we miss the mark.

Even when we turn to God as an image
or concept
or idea,
we miss the mark.

This is what separates the mystics
and the literal minded religious.
At this point, too,
the mystics sometimes flounder.

Turning to God
in the sense of
absolute stillness, in the sense that
one dwells in the great void
cannot be described. But it is here
that we enter fully
into the experience. It is here
that the words
void
or emptiness
take their meaning and significance
for the seeker.
The knowledge
of higher presence
of the ever-present merging
of one ordinary,
small
existence
with a limitless force
comes together.
All the words merge
and disappear
at this moment.

IX in the marketplace

The Ten Oxherding Pictures

I Searching for the Ox
the Boy has only vague presentiments of it's existence

II Finding the tracks
in writings and in teachings he begins to get clues

III Seeing the Ox
he begins to have a glimpse of his own hidden reality

IV Catching the Ox
but owing to the pressures of the World he both catches and loses

V Herding the Ox
even without chains, without his whip, he has never really been apart from the Ox

VI Coming Home on the Ox's Back, he tunefully and leisurely plays his Flute

VII Lo, the Ox is no more the Boys whip and rope idly lying about—not needed

VIII Gone, Gone, altogether Gone, the Boy and the Ox are both 6 one

IX Back to the Source
he is neither for nor against the transformations that are going on

X The Old Man in the Market
no glimpses of the inner life are to be caught—Barefooted he goes to the Market place

172 West 94th Street
New York 25, New York
June 16, 1954

Dear Mr. Segal,

Thank you for your letter of June 11th.
Thank you very much for the printing of the
TEN OX-HERDING PICTURES. As soon as I finish
my new comments on these pictures they will
be submitted to you for approval.

I shall telephone you sometime next week
perhaps about seeing you and your family.

With all best wishes,

Sin cerely yours,

Daisetz T. Suzuki

The Ten Oxherding Pictures

"He enters the city with bliss bestowing hands"

– D.T. Suzuki

The first time my husband and I went to Japan together, in 1973, we visited Roshi Nanrei Kobori, Abbot of the Ryoko-in Temple at Daitokuji monastery in Kyoto. This elegant Roshi, who was a Zen master, a poet and a painter, had just finished a series of ten watercolors called "The Ten Oxherding Pictures." He said to my husband with a smile, "your own version of "The Ten Oxherding," which you showed me in New York, is the first one I know of the old man with western eyes." Bill loved that symbol and he painted it several times.

The Oxherding pictures were first painted in the eleventh century in China. They symbolize the search of a human being for understanding. They depict the spiritual development of a young man over the course of his life. They begin with the boy who has stirrings of aspiration inside of himself. He feels that there is something of significance to be found. He sets off in search of it. He realizes that in order to come in touch with the ox—his inner life—he needs to develop a quality of attention, of work ethics and right relationship with himself and with others. The series shows the different stages until finally the man is in control.

Kakuan, Zen master of the Sung dynasty, had written commentaries and painted a series of pictures focusing on the difficulty of understanding by words alone. The ten pictures show that a man's search can stop neither in emptiness nor in Nirvana (as represented by the circle) and that the seeker must come back into the world and be with others. For, as Kakuan would say, detachment and compassion, as well as time and eternity, are not incompatible terms, it is not this or that, but this and that.

WCS and Kobori Roshi   1960

1980

Going his own way, Bill took liberties in his artistic rendering of the Ten Oxherding Pictures and did not always follow the Zen traditional sequence. In this lithography, the usual number VIII becomes number X as a larger "enso" circle, more harmonious in the middle of the composition. He had planned to enlarge it and started a macro size version in Paris. Sometimes he sketched only human silhouettes, changing their density in the progression. He made multiple sketches showing various transformations.

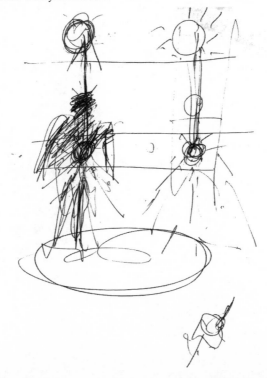

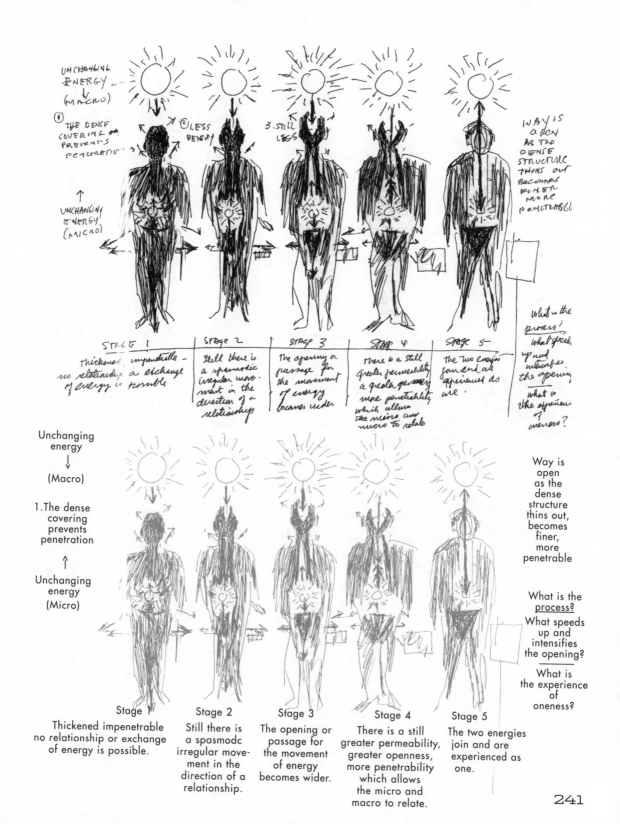

Unchanging
energy
↓
(Macro)

1. The dense
covering
prevents
penetration

↑
Unchanging
energy
(Micro)

Way is
open
as the
dense
structure
thins out,
becomes
finer,
more
penetrable

What is the
<u>process?</u>
What speeds
up and
intensifies
the opening?

What is
the experience
of
oneness?

Stage 1
Thickened impenetrable
no relationship or exchange
of energy is possible.

Stage 2
Still there is
a spasmodc
irregular move-
ment in the
direction of a
relationship.

Stage 3
The opening or
passage for
the movement
of energy
becomes wider.

Stage 4
There is a still
greater permeability,
greater openness,
more penetrability
which allows
the micro and
macro to relate.

Stage 5
The two energies
join and are
experienced as
one.

241

My prayer is to die underneath the
Blossoming cherry,
In that spring month of flowers,
When the moon is full.

Saigyo

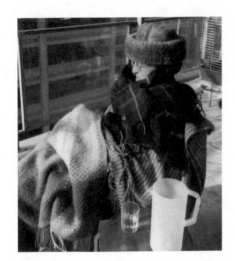

Practicing Emptiness

"I am practicing emptiness," he said softly. "I am eating emptiness. It purifies." He was sitting in his usual chair, basking as he always liked to do in the blazing spring sunshine that was streaming in the window, this time his frail body wrapped tightly in a blanket, a wool hat covering his head despite the warmth of the day. Everything was the same and everything was different. It was May 2000 and the nearly ninety-six year old William Segal was dying. "I want nothing," he whispered, his voice clearly weakening, his gaze steady but remote. "I want no-thing. Just to remain in the middle between the two worlds." And a little while later: "What dream are we in the midst of . . . ?"

Marielle called the day before—a Friday—just as we were coming to the end of yet another screening of the unfinished final film in our trilogy of films on William Segal. We were close, but something in the film—called *In the Marketplace*—was resisting completion. We welcomed Marielle's interruption, but her voice was filled with concern. Bill was not well, she said. But he had been up and down, unwell, for a couple of years. This was nothing new. I promised her that I would come to the city in the middle of the next week, hung up and returned to the film. But as we argued about which scenes could go, which could be trimmed, and which just needed work, I was suddenly overwhelmed by a sense of love for my friend William Segal. I cancelled the rest of the day's work, called Marielle and told her I would be there as fast as I could, in three or four hours.

I first met William Segal more than twenty-five years before in a church basement in Boston. Several of us were sitting on the floor, practicing drawing, doing movements with a brush on paper, trying to bring more attention to the moment. I was struggling, my own feeble attempts at presence, at silence, drowned out by the cacophony of the ordinary mind's chatter. Then, I felt someone standing over me. I turned around and looked up. It was Mr. Segal. In that moment, he saw everything, took me in completely, without judgment or condescension. He smiled and said, "Try again." I made another attempt. This time in a gift sponsored by this remarkable man, the movement I made was effortless, and I felt a calm and sense of being that I had never experienced before. I looked back at Mr. Segal. He smiled, nodded, turned and walked away. I would not see him for some time, but that experience stayed with me, pure and unambiguous, and it would serve as my talisman during years of struggle.

Many years later, I attended an exhibition of paintings and drawings by William Segal. Walking through the gallery I was struck by the force and luminosity of his work, particularly a magnificent self-portrait that I subsequently learned was not for sale. After negotiations, I was able to obtain this extraordinary painting and hang it in my New Hampshire home. Each morning at dawn, I pad downstairs to find, just to the right as I take the last step, this compelling face staring at me, demanding once again my full attention. "Good morning, Mr. Segal," I say each day without fail, grateful for the graceful reminder of a wondrous hidden world, a presence, seemingly so far away and yet so close to the sleep we call our normal "waking" lives.

During the last decade of his life, I had the good fortune to become a friend of William Segal and his beloved wife, Marielle. We collaborated on three short films that help impart Bill's teaching. The first was on his painting and the window it provided to another awareness, the silence he was always seeking. The second film explored the question of search, using the great basilica at Vezelay, France as a stepping stone to an inward, individual journey. The final film, the one that we were struggling with when Marielle called, was on Mr. Segal's interpretation of the Zen/Ox-herding pictures. These drawings detail one man's search for enlightenment and the necessity of bringing that light, as William Segal did, into our ordinary lives—into the marketplace.

When I arrived at his apartment in New York, it was clear that Mr. Segal was indeed between two worlds. His body was failing. He was unable to speak more than a few precious words at a time. But he was all there, still staring out fiercely through those wonderful eyes of his, still completely himself. It seemed to those of us blessed to be sharing this transition with him, that he had always been himself. He was the most authentic human being I have ever met, never trapped by his role of teacher, his light always on, his last moments on this earth as concerned as ever with what those of us helplessly looking on were feeling as he faced his own impending "emptiness." We cried. He joked with us, quoting his friend Georges Duby: "The Earl can bare no more."

After a few days, he stopped speaking all together. But he stayed with us, alert and generous, until he took his last breath on a Tuesday morning, as May flowers bloomed and with the moon nearly full. William Segal was a good man. As his wife Marielle said, "There must be a God to create a human being like that."

Eventually, I went home and finished the final film on Bill's life. By then its problems had all but dissolved. But the memory and imprint of this elegant man lingers, transforming us still. I often recall a favorite passage of his from King Lear:

> I have a journey, sir, shortly to go;
> My master calls me, I must not say no.
> The weight of his sad time we must obey;
> Speak what we feel, not what we ought to say.
> The oldest hath borne most:
> We that are young
> Shall never see so much, nor live so long.

—Ken Burns
Walpole, New Hampshire

The Man in the Marketplace

A Conversation with Ken Burns

KB: In the ox-herding pictures, why is the marketplace the last image?

WCS: In the end, it is the people that count. And it's people that make or break the quality of our lives. Without people, nature is not quite enough. Nature is beautiful in itself, and nature should be in accordance with people. But people who give off a certain vibration, a certain energy interacting with each other, produce something special. In Paris especially there are a great many very energetic, talented, intelligent people. It affects the quality of life all around us.

KB: We recognize in nature, we recognize in the monastic pursuit, some kind of marshaling of energies, and yet, I think I'm hearing you say that that's not enough.

WCS: There is this moment when one is gathering and then one is giving. The difficulty is that, not knowing ourselves sufficiently, we're unable to align energies to the extent of sharing what's truly valuable. Unfortunately, most of our energies are lopsided, too. We're either too much in the head, too much feeling, too much body movement. During monastic training people learn to bring the different energies together. In life, we're usually too emotional or too intellectual, so there's not the proper harmony of energies.

KB: I'm drawn in the city to powerful energies.

WCS: Yes.

KB: And yet there seems to be a danger, too. There's a danger of being lost. Of being manipulated by the city. Do you feel this?

WCS: To a degree we are always being manipulated. Very few of us are so-called masters of our fate. We're moved by impulse. We're moved by suggestion. We are all subject to mechanicalities. There would be much better relationships among people if they could bring a harmony of energy, a totality of energy instead of flying off the handle here, or being smarter than the other fellow there. This is what I think is spoiling many of our relationships. But the city itself, at the same time, feeds. The trick here is to know how to eat the energies which are all around us.

Roger Sherman, Buddy Squires and Ken Burns

KB: How do we begin to transform that energy? How do we eat the energy instead of being eaten by it?

WCS: It all comes down to a question of being attentive, of giving one's attention to this moment, of being in touch with the body, knowing that the feet are touching the floor, and being aware of the onset of emotion. Always to be attentively watching. This attention tends to bring energy patterns together.

KB: It seems quite a difficult discipline to have the inner looking, the looking in towards those emotions and thoughts, but also be able to take in the noise of the traffic and the impressions of the city constantly bombarding one.

WCS: It's a question of being open to these energies, at the same time not to be taken by them too much. In other words, this energy tends to focus.

KB: It seems to me that the city is where we might take our preparation and practice our inner work, but it's very important to have an outer work, is it not?

WCS: The whole secret in life, whether it's inner or outer work, is to give total attention to what one is doing now. If people would concentrate and really look and see how they're working and give their total interest and attention to the moment or to the task at hand, it would make people more effective in living. It would feed them instead of depleting them. Generally we come back over and over again to the necessity of being here as totally as possible, no matter what you are doing. But we do need, also, engagement of the outer world. We need engagement of ourselves with others, and with confrontations. Life is a question of challenge and response.

KB: So the city is the marketplace of challenge.

WCS: The city especially. Of course one can have a wonderful rapport with work whether one is on a farm or whether one is meditating. The question is to give one's wholehearted attention. We don't understand this, we don't understand ourselves, we don't understand how we are subject to influences, we don't understand how we react mechanically, and we are not in touch with the potentialities of energies which are hidden in each one of us. One may have moments of "Oh, this is what is meant by being whole, even holy." It's meant to be here. Then, when everything is important, there is no inner, there is no outer.

KB: How does the city feed you?

WCS: This city, particularly, is so, for me, beautiful, harmonious. I don't know who's responsible, I suppose the early architects who laid out the streets and who guided the buildings. At the time much of Paris was built, mainly the nineteenth century, there wasn't this haste, this lust for money, profits, the bottom line. The workingmen really knew how to work. Materials were honest, they were not synthetic as they are today and there was a vision, evidently, on the part of a few individuals. It's the work of intelligence and feeling, and it is a great work.

KB: How do you practice as you walk down a city street, what do you do?

WCS: One doesn't do anything. One just strives to be open to what's around. To be open. That means you're in touch with the breathing, in touch with the body, in

"One doesn't do anything."

247

touch with the influx of impressions. Most of the time we don't avail ourselves of the wonderful array of impressions which come in through the vision, through hearing, through sensing. All of this is here as if the good Lord made us to take in very fine foods beside the food we eat and the air we breathe. But sometimes, if I am so much in myself I cover up this gift, I am closed and I don't receive what is rightfully the human due.

KB: There's stress in the city, too. It works on us in other ways.

WCS: Yes, indeed. Especially during these special times. The whole earth seems to be under stress. More war, more antagonisms, more hate, more everything. One is compelled to defend oneself, I mean not to waste one's energy in antagonistic attitudes, but to be able to say "no," when "no" has to be said. And to say "yes," and to not be imposed upon, at the same time not to impose on others. It was well put here: "I know how to take my anger out of my pocket." When I want to be angry, I can. I can act angry and defend myself, but interiorly, I'm not angry. Interiorly, I am free.

KB: Let's go back to the idea that the city is where I practice and the whole ox-herding pictures of the search we've pursued ends up in the marketplace. Why do we end up in the city?

WCS: Because, again, it comes down to the fact that within each individual human being, there is this spark of the divine. But we have been trained to ignore it. We don't know how to be in touch with it, except in special moments. Now, when one is in the marketplace, one realizes that behind all the haggling and behind the bargaining and the shouting and the fuss, it gives the possibility of seeing the sacred in every human being and in every piece of fruit and every shouting merchant. So instead of being drained of energy, one is left open to receive and, in turn, this communicates in a strange way. If you're calm and blissful in the marketplace, wherever you go you spread harmony. It really does work for people.

KB: So it's not enough as we pursue this question of search "Who am I?" to stay within the realm of the precious, in the monasteries, in the cathedrals.

WCS: Oh, no. Absolutely not. This is not my way of thinking. I think finally all religions, all ways, lead through life itself. No discrimination between the monastery, the church or synagogues and life itself. This way, where you're sitting and where I'm sitting can be a sacred place. In a certain sense, there's a vibration which can change this place where we are sitting. If we knew better, the world would change. And maybe this is what is meant by the idea that unless there are ten conscious men, the world is going to be in difficulties.

KB: And so I need to bring my practice to the city.

WCS: Yes. Now it comes down to a question of what makes life more meaningful. This is what we're really here for. We're here for something but we don't know for what we're here. We do know that we're bound to experience periods of suffering, of stress, of joy and of happiness. So, when I say, to make life more meaningful, it becomes a serious question. I believe that life becomes more meaningful when one is present to this moment. It sounds so simple, but as soon as I look at you, I see something quite different from what I would ordinarily see when I give you a passing glance. Again, we come back to the idea of relationships. I don't know how to convey this to others but again, let's go back to the city itself, which is a miracle of harmony, color and light.

KB: We were saying that the contemplative, the inward-looking is not enough. That the city provides us with something.

WCS: It is just like friction provides light, energy and force. In the same way, rubbing against other people, meeting situations, overcoming difficulties is all part of making life more meaningful. If I retire into my little ivory tower, what good am I? As one says, it's prepara-

tion, the monastic life, the retiring life, the contemplative life, they're very important periods. However, one must also acknowledge that most people never stop, they don't know the immensity of the moment of stop. If one paused for a moment, one would change many things in the midst of the hurly-burly game of life. But it's also true that people have difficulty making a living and relating in an amicable way with one another. All of life is a challenge which has to be met and one can't meet it without being in the marketplace.

KB: The city is about practice.

WCS: The city is about living. If one says practice is living, the city is where the game is really serious. You can't get away from the city itself. A city provides opportunities to test oneself, too. And to share.

KB: The city does remind me that I can't do it alone.

WCS: The city is a miraculous conglomeration of forces. It's people who develop and who exude vibrations and energies. I remember that one day I was talking to P.D. Ouspensky, and I said, "Why don't you move out? Why don't people move out to the West, where we could have a lot of land, in the desert?" And he answered, "No, it takes hundreds of years to build, to make a deposit of vibrations in a particular place and one can only have this in cities." There must be some reason why locations such as Paris, New York, Tokyo, London are great centers of civilization. Jerusalem, Rome, Athens were deposits of energy coming from people. And then, as they decay, one sees the way the energy moves to other places. There must be some great cosmic scheme, too, which dictates that Paris and New York are special.

KB: And it's important, it seems, to have my own outer work.

WCS: Yes. I was also a magazine maker and a painter, and I suppose unless we're engaged, life is pretty dull, isn't it? You can't just sit around and contemplate your navel. Without occupations, we're pretty much lost. Unfortunately, we're coming into an era where we're sitting in front of the TV, not engaging ourselves enough. We're too passive. The right balance between passivity and action is important. One should be engaged. What you do always feeds you. You're never bored. Some energy appears that we didn't believe existed.

KB: So you see the city as not so much a place of things as a place of opportunities.

WCS: Things are the medium with which we exchange impressions, thoughts, even quarrels. Things are important. After all, man has always been a maker of things, hasn't he? When one goes literally to the marketplace, one sees presentations of fruits and vegetables and fish and fowl. This means there's an innate, an inborn drive towards the aesthetic. Even the humblest grocery store-keeper wants to arrange the fruit just so. Observe a fish market, the way the man places his fish and his oysters. Throughout the marketplace I see signs of this impulse towards beauty.

KB: What is the difference between the way the city wakes you up and the way the country or nature or con-templation does?

WCS: The rate of vibrations that is present in the city is much quicker than the vibrations which are developed in the country, which has it's own tempo. Everything should be in harmony. The city provides the battle-ground of clashing personalities, of opposite mentalities rubbing against each other, towards developing of ener-gies, potentially towards the uncovering of the supreme energy which is not enough present in our lives. But sometimes in the midst of a stressful period, one is brought to a halt and one takes a breath differently, looks around and has another feeling for a mysterious quality which is also present, which probably is connect-ed with the impulse towards the sacred.

KB: Do you think of the city as the place where we leave these deposits that Mr. Ouspensky said?

WCS: I think that the city is a visible deposit of what we have been and what we wish to be. It's so strange to see the difference between a city like New York and the city of Paris. Individualities in New York are so apparent, everybody builds his own way, his own materials, his own heights, whereas in Paris, they were more in conformity with the general principles of harmony, order, let's call it friendly relationships. In New York, I'd put up my own building and I don't care what your building is next to me. There's a big difference there. The Romans built as if they were going to live forever, solid buildings, solid roads, whereas we put up shoddy structures.

KB: The city reminds us of ever-present question of time. Something timeless.

WCS: It's true. Every move we make, every thought we have, leaves a deposit. Unfortunately our perceptions are unable to grasp the fact that this room is filled with materials. Sometimes we do have an intuition about places, streets, buildings, rooms, and we sense the difference between one atmosphere and another. That's very apparent if you went into a jail. It's quite different from going into a church. Some streets are menacing, others are calming.

KB: You were just saying perhaps we can see . . .

WCS: Perhaps we can look at the city as a place where people come together to compete in a fraternal way even though it may sometimes develop into antagonisms. This competition very often tends to bring out the best as well as the worst in people. In one sense, it is a place where one sharpens one's capacities. So from that point of view the city can have a beneficent effect on relationships. One learns to judge what's necessary and what's not necessary. So many of our moves, our attitudes, our actions are not really necessary.

KB: I'm bombarded in the city with so many impressions. How is one's attention able to be appropriate to all of them?

WCS: When you are attentive to the moment, there is a natural selection or rejection of impressions which makes you more open. There's an in-built censorship in relation to impressions. This is where one's intention could be important. If I decide to concentrate now, I become more open to the better quality vibrations.

KB: Let's be practical about this question of intention. I put on my coat and my scarf and my hat and I go out into the city. How can I be at that moment? What are the tricks of the trade?

WCS: That's a good question. With intention, there would certainly be less loss of energy. With intention, one focuses one's capacities, one's reservoirs towards the accomplishment. With intention, one leads a more harmonious existence. With intention, one remembers that there's more to life, more in life than the mechanical associative actions and thoughts to which we're subject for most of the time. One pauses and in this stop, there's a great in-gathering which can help to change life.

KB: I have a sense that what you're saying is that in something as simple as going to the market could be as profound as the most sacred religious...

WCS: Absolutely. Because, after all, one goes to church to be open to the atmosphere and to receive impressions of a very fine order. At the same time, there is the marketplace full of harmony and color and light and activity, very important in developing one's inner life.

KB: It sounds as if you are talking about something joyous.

WCS: Life is joyous.

Article by D.T. Suzuki, originally published in *Gentry*

The Hands

"The illness of modern man comes mostly from his forgetting the loving and inspiring and creative use of the hands."

In the beginningless beginning, that is, when there was yet no time, Spirit thought, "Why not embody myself in some form instead of staying all alone in the solitariness of absolute self?" With this thought, the whole universe in all its multitudinousness came into existence. Spirit was no more itself in its naked spirituality. It had form now, and form is infinitely varied and functions in infinitely varied ways. Man, as one of these forms, appeared with consciousness, and consciousness came with hands. Human consciousness is Spirit individualized and mirrors the later in itself. The hands are the instrument with which Spirit works and goes on creating. The above is the metaphysical way of explaining the world and consciousness.

Consciousness was, perhaps, awakened in man when he began to use the hands to satisfy something more than mere physical needs. As long as man was bound to earth and could not make free creative use of his hands, he had nothing to distinguish himself from other living beings. He could not create.

In the course of evolution, man managed to free his hands from the earth and use them as tools with which he could, in turn fashion things into other tools. In time the hands, together with the arms, acquired efficiency, which meant fingers were differentiated.

The rise of consciousness, I surmise, was simultaneous with the hands' ultimate separation from the earth. Acquiring consciousness, man separated himself from brute existence. The transition meant that man henceforth molded vessels not only for eating and drinking, but concerned himself as well with the shaping of urns and bowls that were beautiful to look at.

Hands and consciousness continued to function together. Hands were sharpened and man had all kinds of cutting machines. Hands were lengthened, and man reached suns and moons and scraped the heavens. Hands increased in sensitivity and man probed the secret of existence.

While technology symbolizes the scientific and the utilitarian aspect of hands, the totality of the significance of hands is not exhausted. Hands still retain and communicate the essence of Spirit. For it is hands alone that create objects of art. Even language embodies a hand function, since it lives as a consequence of being inscribed on papyrus or stone.

Machines, on the other hand, are functions of the intellect—not Spirit. They generalize and impersonalize. No works of art are products of the machine. When hands are converted into machines, they cease to be creative in the true sense, because they become inpersonal. Intellectualization and creativity do not make a good team. When the artist goes beyond the brush, the chisel and the wheel, his products no longer reflect his personality, his creative originality. Technical skill does not constitute the beautiful.

Modern man is too intellectual, too sophisticated, too specialized, too generalized. In him there is too little of the primal man. This is to say that he has forgotten how to use his hands creatively in his daily life. True, he picks up his pen, he writes out his bills, he handles his mechanical devices, but he has no urge to discover in these acts something which leads to the revelation of his inner self.

Seeing is perhaps the most intellectual of our sensory acts; hearing comes next. But both are localized, and represent only partially the emotional fabric of the whole man. While touch is concentrated in the hands, especially in the finger tips, it is diffused over the body. Touch thus symbolizes the totality of man's sense of his physical being. There is something basic and primeval in touch; seeing and hearing are only the differentiations of this sense. To be aware of the reality of what he sees and hears, man must finally touch the object and directly testify to its solidity and authenticity. Hands are thus both passive and active, receptive and aggressive, impressive and expressive. They strew flowers and pearls; they also get stained with blood.

Something not fully revealed must emanate from the hands, for they are often used in healing. A pure man's hands are placed over the patient and he is healed. They are also the instrument of blessing. They perform the office of liaison interpersonal. God's healing and loving and guiding hand moves through our human hand. God's hand is no more than our own. We, however, forget the truth quite frequently and soil ours.

The eye observes and surveys; the ear listens and warns. But it is the hand that stretches out, reaches and grasps.

Somewhere it is written: "Go out into the darkness and put your hand into the hand of God. That shall be better to you than light and safer than a known way."

In a metaphorical sense, the hand points both outward and inward. Outward is light, and inward is darkness. The known way is the intellect, the unknown is creative Spirit. Turn your hand inward and grope in the night of self-consciousness. There your hand touches another hand extended to you. You take it and it leads you "toward the hills and the breaking of day in the lone East."

The noted Japanese Zen master, Hakuin, used to produce his hand and ask his disciples "to hear the sound of one hand." This one hand is the "hand of God stretched out in the darkness." When a man takes hold of it, he can hear the sound of one hand.

A Zen master of the Sung dynasty, Woryo, tried his followers with a threefold question, one of which was: "How much does my hand resemble the hand of Buddha?" He gave his own answer, "A man plays a lute in the moonlight."

What kind of hand is this? Buddha was not a musician, and no one anywhere heard of him playing the lute. Nor was the Chinese Zen master an expert in the art. When the unseen lute-playing hand is seen, we can perhaps also hear the sound of Hakuin's one hand.

I am turning mystical, I am afraid, but actually our everyday life if full of mysticism, full of poetry, because you "hold infinity in the palm of your hand, and eternity in an hour." But there are no such finely drawn mysteries in machinery, in intellectual analysis, in utilitarianism, in technology . . . in other words, in what constitutes the modernity of modern life.

Again, from William Blake: "Tools were made and born with hands, every farmer understands." Tools are hands and hands are tools. But when the hands are not doing anything more than pushing a button, they cease to be hands and tools. They are then no more than an insignificant part of a dehumanizing machine. With such mechanized hands neither husbandry nor handiwork, each in its higher and creative sense, can be performed.

Hyakujo Ekai, of the T'ang dynasty, was the founder of the Zen monastery which properly established Zen Buddhism as an independent form of monastic life. His motto was, "One day of no work is one day of no eating." Faithful to this maxim, he worked with the monks on the monastery farm. The monks, however, did not wish to see their master, old as he was, laboring with the young and strong husbandmen. As the master would never yield to their objections, they hid the farming tools from him. Then Hyakujo said, "If I am not permitted to work there will be no eating for me."

But there is a deeper meaning in Hyakujo's action. It was not a matter of economic principle. He wanted to teach his disciples that there is much more in handiwork than the economics of production. The hands deal always with concrete particulars embodying personality.

Kwannon, usually regarded as the goddess of mercy, is represented with one thousand arms or hands and each one of them carries a symbolic emblem. The hands are meant for creation born of love-consciousness. The illness of modern man mostly comes from his forgetting the loving and inspiring and creative use of the hands.

Conversation with His Holiness the Dalai Lama

William Segal: Thank you for letting us visit you. May I ask a question or two? We have a feeling in the West that, despite difficulties, there is a growing undercurrent of a world coming together. My question would be: how do you see the part that you and the Tibetan people may play in the future—on the spiritual as well as the temporal plane? The West is at the point where it values and understands what the East has to offer. You have probably heard this many times. In a strange way, the Tibetan people are in a unique position in this regard. I don't know how you see this—whether it is a dream, an impossibility?

His Holiness: (laughs) Yes, that is difficult to say. Anyway, yes, everybody, whether Eastern or Western, everybody wants peace and happiness. And nobody wants suffering. There is a feeling of this, yes, in our country. Many people try their best in various tasks, mainly in scientific areas seeking material progress. But there are still many, many problems in the world—insurmountable problems—including mental problems, political problems—although we have had many advances which brought benefit on the material level. Do you get my meaning?

WCS: Yes.

HH: But this mental trouble or mental unrest is still growing.

WCS: The difficulty is there.

HH: So you see, for this mental unrest that afflicts people, for this, the only hope is in the controlled mind. Unless you control your mind there is no individual or world peace. That is how I see it.

WCS: What do you mean by "controlled mind?" The controlled mind in relation to exterior achievement is well understood by the West. In other words, the study—penetration into many technologies is already the province of the Western mind. But is the control of the mind I think you are speaking of something else?

HH: All beings have two qualities: bad qualities as well as good qualities. If the mind has developed bad qualities like hatred, there is bad karma. Kindness, honesty, sincerity—these are good qualities. If one develops good qualities, if there is sincerity, honesty, then everybody realizes that that person is a good person. If one developes the bad side – becomes angry, people realize that he is difficult to deal with and then they try to avoid him, and, sooner or later, violence comes.

Now if we want peace . . . for instance, if there is one family, generally speaking and all members of the family are more or less honest and sincere, then there is true peace within and good relations with neighbors. The result is that the whole village will be united in a good, friendly atmosphere. If one develops bad qualities, then he himself loses and his neighbors also lose. It is worthwhile and necessary to try to develop good qualities, and it is very important to control bad qualities. It is possible to control the mind in this way.

WCS: I think everyone would agree with you that it is desirable to control the mind in the way you put it. But the question remains "how?" How it will be done?

HH: It can be done by various methods. There are many, many such methods. I think all major world religions taught them. For instance, in Buddhism there are certain methods for intellectuals, and others for not such high intellectuals. There are many different levels, different capacities of understanding. For each category, there are various methods.

WCS: Do you think the capacity to hold attention could be developed in people? I know that the Tibetans emphasize meditation, study. Now, are these towards the purpose of holding a certain vibration of attention . . .

HH: Vibration?

WCS: . . . in the sense of an influence? As you said before: if you are kind, then others will be kind. If one man in the village is truly sincere, he influences the whole village. And the question that we ask ourselves in the West is, "how will this change come?" How will it be brought about? Because we all agree with the ideal, but we don't seem to be able to maintain attitudes of good will and kindness. Why is that? Why is it not possible to maintain this more? In other words, I would like to be, have a certain . . .

HH: Yes.

WCS: . . . attitude . . .

HH: Yes, yes, one person's attitude and influence does affect the other, but only to a certain extent. The main thing depends on one's self. Control of the mind or real peace—permanent peace, limitless peace—depends on one's self. If you try, your practice brings something. You cannot get peace—a good result—through someone else.

WCS: Yes. Is there a special influence the Tibetans could bring?

HH: For many centuries, twenty centuries, many nations have tried. Although it is not right to say there has only been failure . . . what has been the result? From our point of view, we emphasize the Dharma, the practice of our spiritual teachings. Buddhism is very deep, very wide. At every point there is a reason. Even for understanding death, there is reason. Without reason you cannot accept any teaching.

WCS: Yes.

HH: Buddhism gives real explanations, not just idealism or fantasy, but the fact. For instance the nature of mind as emptiness, this teaching is very suitable for the scientific mind.

WCS: Yes, there is no question that there has been a tremendous acceptance of Buddhism in the West. I spoke last month to Mr. Asahina, the Japanese roshi, and he speaks the same way as you about the necessity of having a deeper relation with the inner world, with the mind. At the same time, although men of good will, all over the world, accept this, we still have this strife and trouble and discord. Do you think progress is being made? Are we coming any closer to agreement among ourselves? And can Tibet play any special role? That is my question.

HH: Buddhism can certainly play a special role, since it is the "science of the mind" we all need. And we have the complete forms of original Buddhism still working in Tibet. And we can teach it to all kinds of people. In Ceylon, Thailand, there are very good Buddhists. I admire their real saints. In Japan, Korea and some parts of China, there are also many Mahayanian Buddhists. But there are very few Tantric Buddhists outside of Tibet.

WCS: Is there no equivalent of Tantra in Japan?

HH: The Shingon School has three of the four main forms of Tantra, but not the unexcelled Yoga level, with its profound depth psychology and powerful practices.

WCS: There is no practice of this fourth type anywhere but in Tibet—is that what you are saying?

HH: Maybe among some very saintly hermits.

WCS: Only among the hermits?

HH: This I don't know. A few individuals may have this unexcelled practice naturally, but generally, no. Now, in Tibet we have full monastic ethics of Vinaya, every main philosophy and also all methodologies. In monastic Buddhism we have full bhikshu monk vows as in Theradeva countries. There are only small differences between us and Theradeva monks, like the color of robes. No important difference.

WCS: Not much difference.

HH: Right. And as for our philosophy, we have all the same texts and reasoning practices, as well as critical wisdom. Then we have vast teachings of Mahakarma, great compassion, same as Mahayana Buddhists. Do you know about it?

WCS: Yes, I know.

HH: Great compassion. Great compassion. And love for others, sacrifice, compassion, the feeling of other's pain. We fully practice the Mahayana teachings. In China, Korea and Japan, they have the same practice. Now all these things we have. On top of these monastic and Mahayana teachings, we have complete Tantric arts and science.

WCS: I see.

HH: You see, it is a marvelous thing that one person can practice all these teachings together, can combine them. Some people, for instance, some Buddhists belonging to monastic sects do not understand the Mahayana view, Mahayana benefit, the greatness of the Mahayana, and they criticize Mahayana. And some people, some Buddhists who follow Mahayana, they criticize monastic Buddhism. We do not like such divisiveness. We practice everything.

WCS: You include all.

HH: Yes, certain conducts and acts, we are following according to monastic codes. Now for mental practices, we are following the Mahayana. Also we practice Tantric methods—depth psychology, breath yogas, mantric chanting, visualization and subtle body practices.

WCS: Ah . . .

HH: Such things as Kundalini and pranayama, you know? Using the chakras and four chakras of the subtle mind-body system. So to answer your main question about Tibet's potential role in the world today, we can bring to bear on the world's mental problems the full range of original Indian Buddhist arts and sciences. We can reinforce the good efforts of the millions of other Buddhists, help them to avoid divisiveness, and make the Buddhist mind-education accessible more widely to the whole world.

WCS: I understand your point. Now how would you answer a Mahayana zen roshi who says, yes, but our practice of zazen and koan study are fully adequate for understanding? Perhaps it is most important to be able to be—to be here, to be present, with complete attention. Meditating quietly, inner control grows, mind is at peace. What additional quality would you say that Tantra brings?

HH: As I said before, some saintly hermits will find all teachings within themselves. It is a question of the realization of emptiness. All Mahayanists, esoteric or exoteric practitioners accept the wisdom of emptiness. Methods of practice only vary as to speed, depth and intensity; also how they help people access it more easily. It is the most important realization.

WCS: Yes.

HH: Now, how to practice the realization of emptiness. We must realize emptiness if we want to destroy ignorance. We must practice with our mind. When I speak, I use the word "mind" to include all thoughts, all realizations.

Conversation with Dudjom Rinpoche

WCS: At a moment of awareness, I may hear a sort of sound in myself. . .

DR: What sort of a . . . this kind of sound that you get — is it a real sound or is it just a kind of mental impression?

WCS: No. For example, as I speak to you now, I can hear a sound, a vibration, a sort of steady "mmm" (hums) sound. When I am more aware I hear this.

Translator: How you say, this is . . . an actual sound you hear?

WCS: An actual sound.

Translator: As you talk to people?

WCS: When I'm more aware, I hear it. . .when I have more awareness, when my attention is deeper.

Translator: I see.

DR: Yes, in our practice there is a system of training in sound. This may be the sound produced due to your own nervous system and internal energy. But since it helps you to strengthen your awareness, your concentration, it is a good thing and moreover, that some of it, you know, as you hear, has to be looked into as something that has no identity of its own— something that is empty.

WCS: I understand.

DR: Once you are aware of this, it definitely helps in one's spiritual practice.

WCS: Is there any extension of this practice?

DR: To lengthen it, to stabilize it?

WCS: To stabilize at all times . . . it occurs mostly in quiet.

DR: Only when you are very quiet?

WCS: . . . or when there is a sensation of being here.

When there is a presence to a stronger attention.

Translator: Then you get it?

WCS: How to bring it into ordinary moments?

DR: Since this is a sound that is naturally sprung out of emptiness, it is a sign of the progress of inner practice. That means that your practice is going in the right direction and it is all right. So there is nothing specially you can do about it in order to stabilize it, and all that you have to do is just continue as you normally do. Be aware of it without allowing any kind of attachment or a feeling that "this is good" and therefore there is some kind of feeling attachment, or if you feel that this may not be good, there is a feeling of ambivalence. Any such attachment or emotional . . . identification, as you know should not be there.

WCS: Right.

DR: This applies to practice in all its various points. So all that you do is just allow it and just be aware of it and so you see it's all right. But there are other kinds of tremendous progress in each case. For instance, sometimes when practice is really in a good or higher state, then the man working gets the power of seeing things beyond his physical limitations. You know, in other words, something like clairvoyance or clarity or there are things that you hear—things from a distance and that sort of thing. And apart from these mental qualities, you see things which no ordinary mind can see. That sort of thing comes. But whatever practice you do, there should not be any kind of like or dislike, attachments or any kind of, you know feeling of dislike . . . because the practice is for eliminating all kinds of emotional attachment.

WCS: In this connection, I have no wish. I have no intentions. I don't know whether this is right, because in a way, does it not show a lack of feeling? But I'm not so sure . . .

DR: What you are saying is that this may be a trap? But it is a natural result of practice.

WCS: I understand that.

DR: If it is good, well, if you keep your mind in such a state, a balanced state, then if that sound is something not helpful, it will automatically disappear. If it is beneficial and good, it will be there, and it will certainly help focus.

WCS: I understand. Is there a state of total attention? And what would be characteristic of it? In other words without desiring anything, one feels that one is here, simply here. Is there any practice beyond being here, beyond being here as we are at this moment?

(Translator confers with Rinpoche) Tape is interrupted.

DR: You see, this state of mind that is free of emotional imbalances—in which you will gradually reach the state where there are no doubts, no fear, is very free from worldly conflict—whether it is emotional or otherwise. Intellectual doubts and all this. Once you reach that state, this is the one, and there is nothing beyond, this is actually what practice is for.

WCS: I understand and agree.

DR: The ultimate truth is free from all the delusions. Just emptiness. Where there is neither good or bad, in which there is neither expectation nor fear . . . just a total state of emptiness which cannot be described. This being so, we also have the other aspect, which is the manifestation of the ultimate truth, in that things appear, that is, from the relative standpoint and, really that there would be no obstruction between the two—at once you have the ultimate nature of things. That is the manifestation of the ultimate nature of things from the relative standpoint.

Therefore, from the relative standpoint, everything is and everything can be understood in terms of interdependence. Therefore this understanding of these natural things should not prevent you from acting according to what appears to you. For instance, things appear to you, therefore, we have certainly in this a certain sense of understanding, a certain sense of discrimination—a relative standpoint. But our understanding of the relative standpoint should not obstruct us from our understanding of the ultimate nature of things. In other words, these two should be complementary to each other, and this is the ultimate relation. If you say there is nothing—everything is just nothingness—therefore there is no good, no bad, there is no discrimination, no matter what one does, it doesn't matter because everything can be justified—then we are ignoring the relative truth of conventional wisdom . . . but this is also important, because we have our existence. Therefore this should be understood in terms of either ultimate truth or relative truth. These two should be indivisible in any approach.

WCS: Right, very clear, yes. We have a saying which is very close—that time, which is relative, is in love with or connected to eternity, which is timeless. So the two are connected, can go together.

Translator: Yes, yes

WCS: The eternal is in love with the things of time. . . connected with the relative.

Translator: That's true.

WCS: I would like to ask him another question. What could be most helpful to reach this state, this point that he is speaking about? This state of awareness?

(Translator confers with Rinpoche.)

DR: Just as was said earlier, it is available to anybody interested in spiritual practice, which is simple and which is a condensation of many essential points. There is nothing more important and nothing more useful. One should be always aware of the indivisibility of the absolute nature of things, as well as the relative aspect. One tries to understand the ultimate nature of things whether it concerns the mind or things external.

WCS: Can you say that it's usually thinking that stands in the way? Is it the mind, the thinking mind that stands in the way of a direct perception of things? In other words, you speak of a reality of things, and very often we are so busy thinking that we lose the direct perception and nature of things. Can you say something about that?

DR: Your point is, when you are conscious of a thing, your thinking process interferes with your. . .

WCS: . . . direct perception. If I conceptualize this is yellow, this is brown . . . On the other hand, if I am quiet in my mind, I have a direct knowledge of things. What is the part of the mind in all this?

DR: Yes, that's right. Some people . . . *(Tape breaks, translator confers with Rinpoche.)* As was said earlier, the sensory experiences that we have: "I" thinking, "I" hearing, "I" touching—all these experiences are always there. But when you say, for instance, look at the tree—the first moment you come into contact with an external object, you have the sensation of sight or form. But then, immediately, in that second moment, you begin to use your thinking process. Therefore thought takes place. And after that, the likes and dislikes; because in your thinking process you introduce certain ideas, therefore reality-perception stops. Now, in the practice, when you see a thing, instead of allowing the mind to be influenced by ideas and likes and dislikes, you just be more aware of that moment, without allowing the thinking process to interfere. But you also have to be aware of the empty nature of that which appears before you. In that way, these two aspects—the absolute nature and the relative—from our standpoint, they go hand in hand. One does not obstruct the other.

An interview with the Tibetan physician, Dr. Yeshi Dhonden

Sleep and the Inner Landscape

by William and Marielle Segal

William Segal: Shakespeare wrote that sleep "knits up the ravell'd sleave of care." How do you see sleep in a physiological sense?

Dr. Yeshi Dhonden: Because it is strenuous for consciousness to be constantly distracted among the gross objects of experience, the return to the subtle level experienced in sleep is extremely beneficial to the consciousness and its relationship to the physical body. We understand the physical body in terms of five elements: the four elements of earth, air, fire, and water; the fifth element is sometimes space, sometimes consciousness, depending on different systems. In that context, when one is awake, the four elements are extremely active and consciousness is very much mixed among the four elements, and throughout the five external sense powers. Consciousness is distracted by the coarse objects of experience. Therefore when one falls asleep, it is very similar to the death process. That is to say, the six-fold aggregate consciousness, which in its rest stage resides in the heart, withdraws from its sensory activity, and returns into the subtle plane.

WCS: Can you go into the problem of insomnia and the question of "body-mind complex"?

Dr. D: Because of the mind's need to retain its contact with its own subtle levels, it also has the ability through the vehicle of sleep to withdraw from constant involvement with gross-level activity. People who are unable to sleep well are usually under the influence of desire and attachment.

WCS: Sometimes in the waking state one has a clear cognition of one's existence. What happens to the sense of self in sleep, behind all this turmoil and activity which you describe?

Dr. D: The sense of self that we tend to have in the waking state of consciousness is a distorted one. It is a false identification with the coarse objects and elements of experience and the sense realms. When we fall asleep the erroneous delusory sense of self dissolves into what we call the extremely subtle wind-mind, or neural energy mind.

WCS: What is to be learned in sleep? Is there anything which speaks to the unfulfilled needs of the inner psyche which can carry over from sleep to the waking state?

Dr. D: In the Buddhist view, the sleep and death states are similar. The dream state and the between state and the birth state or the rebirth state are similar. So the entire life cycle is encapsulated in the cycle of sleep, dream, and waking. Therefore, since the death state and the sleep state are the same, that is the time when one automatically enters into what the Tibetans call the Clear Light, the experiential description of Ultimate Reality. In death, one passes through the Clear Light in a certain way, usually failing to recognize that Clear Light, and thus immediately getting involved in the Forms of the next life. In the same way, in the sleep state one automatically enters the Clear Light, as experienced by a very subtle wind-mind. But the sleeping person usually cannot recognize where he is because the connection of the coarse mind and subtle mind is not consciously traced by the individual.

WCS: Why do many people feel reluctant to interrupt the state of deep, restful sleep?

Dr. D: It depends on which of the "three poisons," the three major mental addictions or habits, called desire, hatred and delusion, are predominant. The person who is lethargic, who is prone to strong delusion-predominance, will particularly like sleep. Desire-type people and anger-type people will not necessarily be interested in sleep. It depends on their particular tendency.

All this has to do with the cycle of the elements. Particularly in human beings, the elements manifest in regard to what is known as the three humors. These are the wind, the bile and the phlegm. When the phlegmatic humor, which relates to earth and water, increases, then heaviness and stability increase. And that happens at night.

If, in fact, this balance is not observed, and we do not allow this time for the increase of the earth and water elements and do not sleep for long periods of time, then those elements become out of balance and we feel the effects. Therefore, it is essential that one sleeps to keep things in equilibrium.

WCS: Do you place any emphasis on the time of meditation practice before sleep or upon awakening?

Dr. D: There are various levels of meditation. If one is in a stage of intensive meditative practice, the morning is the best time. When one's energies are fresh and when one concentrates on a particular point, meditation is most effective in the early morning.

It is also true that if we meditate at the time of falling asleep, we can keep the continuity of our meditation going better and sleep more refreshed. We can even have auspicious or educative dreams by having a certain concentration near the time of falling asleep. However, for us ordinary people, if we're trying to meditate before falling asleep we may go to sleep while meditating.

WCS: In relation to what you just said about educative dreams, who or what can remember the dreams and the experiences of sleep? When I wake up, I go back to my mind for memory or recall. What level of mind remembers? Who observes all this show? Who remembers the different states?

Dr.D: That is explained in terms of the subtle and the coarse consciousnesses. In other words, that entity which remembers is the subtle consciousness, which is

the person's real consciousness. This subtle consciousness is present as a continuum throughout all of these states and maintains the continuation among these states, as indeed, according to the Tibetan view, it links the different lifetimes of sentient beings. The remember-er is one's subtle consciousness. The coarse self, identified with the body, is not one's real self.

WCS: Some people remember their dreams. Others do not. Why?

Dr. D: The really developed man can be perfectly aware

of all his dreams. He has full mobility between the subtle and the coarse states. His memory is infallible. He can remember every kind of experience, even former lives. But that's another question. However, the reason that ordinary people sometimes do not remember is that although they have the same subtle consciousness, the same Clear Light connection, they do not pay attention to it. They have no context with which to understand what is taking place.

The subtle consciousness is something like an atomic consciousness. It is very, very subtle. Its experience is within the vast landscape of the central inner nervous system. If the subtle consciousness which resides there moves from the central area, this would be experienced as a coarse type of ordinary dream. It is the passage of subtle energy consciousness within the inner landscape. When it goes into the throat area, into the brain area, or into the naval area, there will be other types of experience.

Dreams occurring right after falling asleep reflect the process of digestion, and would be highly irrelevant as far as spiritual growth goes. But dreams at the early predawn time, for example where the system is mostly clear of the evening's food and the channels are more receptive to the passage of the subtle energies, can be very illuminating. Sometimes they reveal the future and other things. Training the mobility of the subtle consciousness and developing a relative mastery of it in its different states, is the way to develop special powers.

WCS: Is there a way which we can have an influence on the powers of dreaming?

Dr. D: The ideal position for sleep, in the sense that it keeps the eight channels balanced, is to lie on the right side in what is known as the "lion posture." It is better not to put pressure on the heart. There is a definite connection between posture and the type of inner landscape travel happening in sleep.

WCS: If there is a different time-space continuum in

sleep and if transformation of energy is continually going on in our lives, how are these transformations related to our time and space?

Dr. D: First, subtle energy-wind-mind never dies, ever. A Buddha essence is in every being. It never disappears. If one body dies, the Buddha essence simply takes up residence in another body. Continuity is maintained through death. However, for ordinary beings, this realization slips by without being noticed either in sleep or in death. It takes up another "between state" and another rebirth. One just shoots right by the realization, hardly noticing the time of complete subtleness when one is really totally in contact with it.

The actual conscious flowering of Buddhahood is the realization that the subtle mind is completely indivisible from the Clear Light Reality, a conscious experience which you could call timeless, infinite or spaceless. Certainly it is beyond the ordinary sense of relativity and of time and space.

There is another interesting point: how do we in our ordinary human bodies on this earthly plane with our physical size and a time sense of a life span of fifty, sixty or hundred years—how do we relate the subtle conscious energy to our reality? In the back of the heart chakra, heart complex, there is a space inside the central channel, a kind of chamber that is usually sealed off in the ordinary person by certain knots in the channels. It is only a Buddha who has it opened. The subtle consciousness energy can go in and out of that chamber and there is no difference between that chamber and the rest of his being. For us, it is a closed-off chamber where there exists something similar to a treasure box. In this resides a drop, another little treasure box, inside of which the jewel is the extremely subtle consciousness.

When an ordinary person dies, these knots unravel and that jewel will travel until it finds another storehouse, another place of residing. For example, in rebirth it enters the drops of the father and mother in the womb of the mother. This little drop carrying this gem of indestructible subtle consciousness will enter the two drops of the father and mother in the womb from the between (or bardo) state. Birth is expressed in the form of the union of the three drops—the white drop of the father, the red drop of the mother, and the blue drop of energy consciousness. The three will combine and that will be rebirth.

WCS: How to open this inner chamber during one's lifetime? Is it a question of discipline and practice? Can we approach it from a physiological point of view?

Dr. D: This consciousness sits in its seat like a jewel within a kind of mandala palace or mansion. It has in itself no obstruction. It can travel anywhere. There is no need to open any doorway, it is completely open. It is perfect in itself. It is home in a way.

WCS: At the same time, mankind is afflicted with suffering and pain. If it is as you say, why isn't the path more readily apparent, more readily available?

Dr. D: This consciousness in the ordinary person is unrecognized. Everyone has it, but no one recognizes that he has it. People identify themselves with their coarse-level consciousness. Even though this subtle level of consciousness is enshrined there, people do not notice it. They can even go through death, where in fact the coarse level of consciousness is dissolved along with the sense-organs and the coarse elements, and still they don't know because they are drawn into creating a new coarse level involvement in the between state and then in the future birth state. That's why in our science of dying—in The Tibetan Book of the Dead—the essential issue is to bring the dying person face to face with the Clear Light Reality, which is to dwell in their subtle reality, to appropriate their own subtle reality as their reality, rather than simply jump off into another coarse reality. Now the way of doing that is not effective for someone who identifies with the gross reality and with his possessions.

In the direct experience of emptiness, the critical

wisdom penetrates, drilling through the apparent solidity of the coarse-level reality, seeing it for its insubstantiality, and ceases therefore to find anything with which to identify. In the process of coming to that true intuitive wisdom, one joins with one's own subtle level consciousness until finally one uses it to know directly the emptiness which is the nature of Ultimate Reality, beyond any coarse intellectual or conceptual consciousness.

When the subtle consciousness, directly from the heart, experiences this emptiness of intrinsic substantiality, then one has achieved one's own Buddhahood. At that time this subtle consciousness, without any interference, can know everything at no matter what distance. That is why it is said that there is no obstruction at all to Buddha's omniscience. Buddha's mind is omniscient because it is the subtle consciousness that can be anywhere without obstruction. And that never dies, that never dies.

WCS: Perhaps all this depends on a sort of continuous awareness and capacity to hold one's attention on what one could say is one's subtle nature. In other words, if one is distracted by body, mind, feelings, one fails to remember this subtle consciousness. Could you verify this?

Dr. D: In general what you say is correct. Basically the essence of Buddhism is not trying to find something one doesn't have, but simply to recover what one does have but doesn't know it. However, one should be clear. What is involved is a difficult process because of the intensity and the type of the distractions. When you say distractions, you are saying a great deal.

The only way to radically pacify distraction on the gross level is not simply to suppress awareness of the gross-level reality. By fully confronting the gross-level reality and looking at it with critical, penetrating wisdom, one sees its true nature. This is not at all a quieting of the mind, but an intensifying of the mind's analytic, penetrating functioning—like a scientific analysis. It is actually an intensifying of the investigating process.

Awareness of the deepest nature is much more involved than a simple suppression of obvious mental manifestations which we would think of as distractions.

WCS: Is it true that all human being are close to Buddhahood?

Dr. D: I certainly think that from the Buddhist point of view the human being is incredibly close to evolutionary perfection, which is called Buddhahood. It is so in the sense that in a single life, if a human being practices assiduously and has the teachings, he can actually transform himself from an ordinary human being into a perfectly enlightened being.

There are many forms of life within the ocean of evolution which have undeveloped brain systems, such as the different types of lower animals. These types are much less suited than human beings for the pursuit of this perfection of enlightenment. That is why Tibetan Buddhism stresses that people use this precious human life to the very fullest to achieve evolutionary perfection, or Buddhahood. To waste this pinnacle of human life rather than to obtain Buddhahood is a tremendous waste. Any system which says that humans cannot understand, that only God or other super-beings can understand, is repressive of the full potential of the human being and does not agree with the Tibetan Buddhist view.

WCS: But the fact of the matter is that the human being faces almost insurmountable odds to achieve the Buddhahood you are speaking of. How would you answer this?

Dr. D: There is no big problem, in fact, to the human being such as people think. If any one individual really decides that this is what he really has to do, he can do it. The obstacle is one of easiness, in a way. For instance, if people are too happy on a superficial level, and if things are too easy for them, indeed there is an obstacle. If they have suffered and experienced the nature of life and death and pain, usually they realize they must do something to develop themselves, and once they have that resolution, no obstacle can withstand their resolve.

WCS: What do you think of the recent Western experiments and investigations into sleep and dreams? What would be a right path to pursue?

Dr. D: EEG, charting waves, measurements of dreams, can only give superficial information. One only learns about the currents which move in the body. It is a vague and unreliable approach which is not particularly exciting. There is no need at all to wear out machinery and brains. There is already an existing record of thousands of years of experimentation. There are thousands of pages cataloguing the different states of sleep and types of dreams. This study would be fruitful for scientists and researchers. There are plenty of these texts in American university libraries. I know these books and where they are. You only need people who can read them. There is nothing in Tibet you don't now have in America. Everything is here.

–Translated by Robert Thurman

WCS, Dr. Dhonden, MBS, Robert Thurman

ACKNOWLEDGMENTS

I wish to pay homage to the original and unconventional minds of Tracy Carns and Fifi Oscard, who both appreciated Bill's many-sided universe at first reading of the manuscript. Thanks to them and to Peter Mayer's openness, this book is published.

With whom should I start? They come together, all these friends whose affection and uninterrupted help deeply moved me, and made me move. First and foremost I thank the trio I unconditionally trust: Peter Brook, who said to me, "Make a beautiful object"; Robert Thurman who repeated with enthusiasm, "Don't cut, Bill was the most avant-garde American, don't cut"; Ken Burns, whose filial love is always present, lately advised, "Begin with pictures. It creates the atmosphere without words."

Indeed there are many pictures, large and small, of great and generous photographers like David Heald, Roger Sherman, Lee Ewing. Many images were also taken by friends attracted by a photogenic subject: Camilla Rockwell, Wendy Conquest, Sarah and Lilly Burns, Masanobu Bekku, Charles Van Maanen, Barbara Ford, Maya Deren, Buddy Squires Barbara Queen, Françoise Legrand, Jean-Philippe Charbonnier, Uta Hoffman, and Elizabeth Segal Katz for the Ten Oxherding Pictures. So many others come to me "en foule". Here I must thank Cornelia Bessie and James George who often translated my too French expressions. I thank Bill's friends who helped me with their time, talent and generosity, in particular Jon Pepper and Barry Svigals; Jim Safarti and Jim Kendrick, both so patient with me while scanning photographs; Bill Bonnell, always bringing advice and a new working cover for each new title; Dan Surak, for remembering the magazines; Shimon Malin, for offering original documents. In various ways I thank Bruno de Panafieu, Michel de Salzmann, J.C. Lubichinsky, Christopher Maggos, Villette Gebhart, Patricia Llosa, Richard Stein, Margaret Croydon, Sherry Holzman, Wendy Bayne, Woody Dorsey, Andrei Serban, Dana

Dima, David McKinnon, Bryan Doerries and Godfrey Howard. Thanks to Carla Needleman for chapter five. And deserving special mention for the chapter on Japan are Stephen Grant and his daughter Natasha who deciphered the hand written letters and Mihoko Okamura-Bekku, who sent all photographs of D.T. Suzuki.

Not least, Mark Magill, close reader of every draft, patient collaborator and skillful reconstructor. Thank you one and all.

—MBS

Loveliest of what I leave behind is the sunlight,
    And loveliest after that, the shining stars and the moon's face,
  but also cucumbers that are ripe, and pears, and apples.
                    —Praxilla of Sicyon, 5th century B.C.